carry me through

carry me through

A 90-DAY DEVOTIONAL FOR WHEN YOU CAN'T GO ON

LINDA S. CLARE

Carry Me Through (For When You Can't Go On)

ISBN: 978-1-61715-554-3 print

978-1-61715-555-0 eBook

First Printing 2026

Manuscript Editing by Write Way, PS Wells, Roanoke, IN

Text design and layout by PerfecType, Nashville, TN

Cover Design by Amber Weigand-Buckley

Printed in the United States of America

Contents

Introduction

Even to your old age and gray hairs I am he, I am he who will sustain you. I have made you and I will carry you; I will sustain you and I will rescue you.
—Isaiah 46:4

From the time I believed in Jesus, I've prayed for miracles. I've asked for a miraculous healing for my polio-paralyzed left arm and hand. I've prayed for my husband's kidneys to heal. And I've worn holes in the carpet pleading for my children's deliverance from substance abuse and mental illness.

Who doesn't want or need a miracle or two? Like many of you, I've blamed my lack of miracles on my puny faith. I've cried myself to sleep begging God to demonstrate the "ask anything in My name and I will do it" verse (John 14:14). I've studied my Bible, attended faith healings, been anointed with oil, and dared to try a couple of other sketchy rituals.

So far, my miracles have been really late.

When I worked in a Christian bookstore, two women once approached and whispered, "God would heal that arm if you had more faith." I was certain the fault lay with me. Every time I tried to pick up a mustard seed's worth of faith, it slipped through my fingers.

But as I sought a jumbo faith, a funny thing happened. I saw how hard it is to live with an *only a miracle will do* attitude. I needed more. I wouldn't last long enough for a miracle to appear. Right that minute, I needed God-sized strength to manage minute-by-minute suffering. I prayed for God to pick me up and hold me close while I mustered the courage to go on. I needed Jesus to carry me in his arms.

Immediately, Jesus answered. I felt swept up into the Lord's arms like a bride carried over a threshold. My circumstances were still the same—differing degrees of awfulness. But as Jesus carried me through the horribleness. I changed.

Don't get me wrong—I hate suffering as much as anyone. But with God as near as breath, I was different. Instead of always begging God to pluck me out of whatever miserable or scary thing I faced, I began to concentrate on the strong arms that somehow got me through to the next disaster. My prayers still included asking for healing miracles, but I didn't limit myself to *either/or* prayer.

And I no longer thought of God in a transactional way, giving my allegiance and love in exchange for God doling out the favors I sought. I no longer cowered in a corner, fearing punishment whenever I believed I had angered God by breaking a rule.

When your whole body aches with pain and exhaustion, with worry and dread, with sorrow and unfathomable grief, your miracle might be late too. Never stop hoping and praying but remember that God's love will never leave or forsake you (Deuteronomy 31:6 and Hebrews 13:5).

I hope you'll feel secure, comforted, and loved as you read these devotions. Let Jesus carry you through whatever you're facing today.

part one

When Bad Stuff Happens, He Carries You

When You Ask God, Why?

Oh, how great are God's riches and wisdom
and knowledge! How impossible it is for us to
understand his decisions and his ways!
—Romans 11:33 (NLT)

Remember the old poem? Jesus walks on the beach beside you, but there is only one set of footprints in the sand. Although it's rather cliché now, it's true. Jesus carries us when life is too hard. I learned this twenty years ago, when my close friend, Patti, died from an aggressive form of breast cancer.

At the time, I prayed fervently and often, asking God to spare Patti's life. Her entire family stormed the gates of heaven with their pleas, even cashing in life insurance policies to help Patti afford a stem cell transplant. During a two-year period, she received the transplant and a host of other cancer treatments.

But despite the supplication and her own fighting spirit, my friend Patti passed away from that dreaded disease.

I felt devastated. I blamed myself for her death and plunged into deep grief and depression. Didn't the Scriptures promise that we could ask anything in faith and God would do it? Scripture also says God doesn't make mistakes. Therefore, I concluded, prayers for Patti's healing must have fallen short due to my imperfect faith.

Most of us have asked *why*. Why, God, did prayers for health not result in healing? Why didn't you give us what we asked for? Why, God, can't we figure out the right level of faith needed to get our desired results? Even with phrases like "it wasn't God's will" or "God's timing is not our timing," losing a loved one hurts. Cuts us to the core. Turns our lives upside down with grief. In fact, sometimes these pat explanations increase suffering and sorrow.

I doubt that God gets mad because we question. My God is bigger than a bunch of human doubts or questions. A loving God doesn't judge me for asking why. But all my whys have led me to a different conclusion: When my prayers aren't answered the way I hoped, Jesus carries me through.

But the Lord doesn't carry me *around* my problems as if there's a detour to avoid. So far, I usually don't get to leap above a challenge or dig down underneath something terrible. Nope. Jesus picks me up, and we go straight through the worst of it. For as long as the journey takes, Jesus is right there with me, buffeted by the same headwinds, lending me strength, determination, and gobs of love.

Whenever you ask, "Why, God?" in the midst of life's calamities, disappointments, or failures, you'll still hurt, grieve, or go through hell itself. Yeah, I hate that too. But look behind you. You'll see one set of footprints if you let Jesus carry you through the storm.

"A man who walks with God always gets to his destination."

—Henrietta C. Mears

When Anxiety Stalks

Cast all your anxiety on him because he cares for you.
—I Peter 5:7

One of my family members suffers from anxiety that's so pronounced, it lands him in the emergency room. When the anxiety starts, he hears buzzing, followed by numbness. He can't speak. His arms and legs contract until he's in a fetal position, unable to move. If anyone tries to unfold his limbs, the pain is excruciating. After a while, the attack passes, and he's able to move once again.

This loved one isn't feigning attacks to get attention. When the buzzy numbness starts, there's a chance he can stop the episode—and he tries. But once his limbs stiffen, he loses control of his muscles. His severe anxiety wins again.

The hardest part is that doctors usually release him, saying, "It's *only* anxiety. Deal with it." Okay. But how?

Most of us *deal* with anxiety by using self-talk or the support of loved ones. Some, like me, anticipate dread by practicing. As a child, I was so anxious about visiting the dentist that I lay in bed the night before, jabbing my gums to be sure I wouldn't scream when the Novocain injection went in. I was willing to suffer twice in my attempt not to look like a baby in front of the dentist.

My childish way of dealing with anxiety didn't help much. The more I worried about tomorrow, the less I could enjoy the now. I wish I'd learned to cast my cares upon Jesus a lot sooner.

Casting our anxieties upon Jesus may not seem as powerful as an anti-anxiety drug or the massage chair at the mall, unless we remember that God is with us every step of the way. I once thought casting my anxiety on the Lord meant to say a prayer and then try really hard not to look nervous. But no matter how many *What? Me worry?* prayers I said, anxiety fluttered in my stomach.

Of course, there's a difference between I-need-a-good-parking-spot anxiety and oh-lawd-I-just-got-the-worst-news anxiety. Yet when we cast our cares on him, it needn't be a last-ditch Hail Mary effort.

Sometimes my loved one can stop those attacks in time. Sometimes the attacks bulldoze over him. Either way, God carries him through. In every situation, hand your cares to Jesus as if he's standing right next to you—because he is. And casting cares shouldn't only mean, "I'll take miracle number two, hold the pickle."

For as much as we wish to escape life's hardest stuff, we can cure our fear immediately by giving God our trembling hearts and letting him carry us through the sewer. *Because he cares for you* isn't just a nice sentiment. Jesus cares enough to carry you through the absolute worst.

"Anxiety's like a rocking chair. It gives you something to do, but it doesn't get you very far."

—Jodi Picoult

When Life's Unfair

"I have told you these things, so that in me you may have peace. In this world you will have trouble. But take heart! I have overcome the world."
—John 16:33

My four children argued over almost everything. Even trickier, two were twins. Birthday cake slices had to be exactly alike. Each had to receive an equal number of presents. When one twin got something more than the other, the cry went up. "No fair!"

I always smiled and paused for a few seconds before I said, "Life's unfair. Get over it." My pronouncement didn't do much to change their ideas about equity, and if I'm honest, I thought the same thing. Life's *so* not fair.

If the God of the universe were all about fairness as we apply the concept, he wouldn't have gifted me with twins in the first place. Some people know that I contracted polio at eight and a half months old. My left arm and hand have been paralyzed since. I type, cook, sweep, and do everything using one hand.

Also, no one expected more than one baby. The whole birth and subsequent years of raising twins came as a complete surprise, even to the attending doctor. As the first baby lay in my arms, the doc exclaimed, "Oh my God, there's another one."

I exclaimed, "Oh my God."

So began one of my most difficult journeys. Caring for my two older sons and two colicky preemies proved daunting. I thought it manifestly unfair to give the one-handed woman two babies, or that God's sense of humor is kind of edgy.

My darlings survived childhood, even though I had to haul them up with one arm to carry them. Oh, the unfairness. I blame it on Jesus.

I'm certainly no saint—just ask anyone back then who heard me pleading for a solid night's sleep. All new parents know *that* kind of unfairness. Yet the more helpless I became, the more I sensed that Someone was carrying me along, getting me through each long day.

As I sat in the rocking chair with them at two a.m., Jesus stayed close by. How else can I explain the praise that welled up in my exhausted baby-body? I sang to my infants, instilling them with God's love, promising they would be strong and courageous. The milk that nourished them was holy, and each star outside the window pointed to the Morningstar himself.

When life's unfair, we can bring our disappointment to the one who can pick us up, not by one arm, and get us to the next stop on our journey. Life will never be fair, but Jesus will carry us through.

If you do one good deed your reward usually is to be set to do another and harder and better one.

—C. S. Lewis

When You're Frazzled

Rescue me, O God! Lord, hurry to my aid!
—Psalm 70:1 TLB

After several days of intense busyness, I flopped into a chair. Everything ached—even my hair hurt. I'd been scurrying around like a crazy squirrel. I took kids to school, did a work project, planned dinner, got to the gym, and picked up the kids. To say I was frazzled was an understatement.

Sometimes life does seem to whiz past, carrying us along. We often take on hectic schedules, overcommitting to one too many activities, telling ourselves we can do it all. Whether you're career-oriented or trying to be your perfect self, being *busy* tops the list.

And we must make those lists to keep that schedule humming along. We smile and act cool, but inside the hamster wheel spins out of control. How do we keep our sanity and still get things done?

I've heard some people approach life more slowly, with less frenzy, but I'm not one of them. I can't sit still for long. My husband once remarked that I'd never sat and watched a full movie with him. During the commercial or the slow bits, I'd pop up to dust the furniture or fix him a snack.

Nervous energy aside, many of us have been taught to keep busy. While the Scriptures have warnings against idleness, I can't find the part that says I must volunteer for every activity in my community. When James says to be a doer and not a hearer only (James 1:22), I doubt God is interested in snappish behavior that arises when we are exhausted.

My husband and I both rate as Type A folks. We go from zero to a hundred in two seconds. While I flit around like a hungry bee, he hates to be interrupted. The man can sit and stare at the computer screen or the TV for hours. When I take my chances and announce that dinner is served, he growls, "What?"

To avoid dumping his food in his lap, I take a deep breath and send up an SOS prayer: *Dear Jesus, please pick me up right this second so I don't break any laws. Because I'm this close to biting off his head.*

But before Jesus even carries me a foot, he convinces me to let out all the hurry. All the frenetic busyness that says, Now! As I allow tension, stress, and terrible thoughts to exit, Jesus shows me how to replace my awful impulses with the same mercy he shows to me.

Maybe it's because bad attitudes weigh so much more than love. When Jesus hoists me up, I can rise to the realm where love lets me slow down and learn what really matters.

"No matter how busy you are, you must take time to make the other person feel important."

—Mary Kay Ash

When Willpower Won't Do

I can do all things through Christ who strengthens me.
—Philippians 4:13 (NKJV)

If you've made a New Year's resolution, you know about willpower. I have vowed to lose weight, go to the gym, start riding the exercise bike, or quit a bad habit.

Soon enough, willpower turns to won't-power.

The first time I blow the diet or sneak that extra dark chocolate, I tell myself I can still succeed. But as soon as January wanes, I admit that I'm losing the resolution battle. And then I try to forget the whole idea.

But I still feel like a loser. Christ didn't strengthen me enough to do all the things, so I whine. And if I keep heaping blame upon my puny faith, nothing will change.

I've made many resolutions that crashed and burned exactly that way. One year, I joined a weight-loss clinic and resolved to lose the extra baby pounds hanging around my hips. I did lose the pounds over a six-week regimen. Yay, me.

Trouble was, the day after the diet program ended, I baked and ate almost an entire chocolate cake. Had Christ not strengthened me? Or had I twisted the Scripture and hitched it to my own willpower?

I admit it was the latter. I thought I could use my faith as a weapon to get what I wanted: a pre-baby body. All I had to do was post the words from Philippians like a stop sign warning me not to cross the calorie limit. Or else.

Combined with a list of legal foods and a counselor who weighed me once a week, strengthening was little more than a deterrent not to break the law. As soon as the choice was my own again, I did what many sleep-deprived new mothers do—I ate and ate and ate.

Back then, I didn't realize that Jesus wanted to help me make good food choices. He's more interested in the kind of strengthening that gives me confidence to eat healthily.

I didn't understand that the Lord doesn't want to be a mean cop, gleefully announcing my failure while subtracting brownie points. Accusation has many voices—our own inner critic and the unkind words of others—each trying to convince us we blew it.

Instead, Jesus shows us a way to be compassionate toward ourselves. He holds onto the back of the bicycle seat until we get going. When we crash on that two-wheeler, he gives the courage to keep trying.

Change is hard, Jesus says. Keeping resolutions can be like riding downhill without brakes. But if we allow him to strengthen our love for God and our neighbor, we can change, even if we fail a hundred times.

If we can stop seeing the Lord as the willpower police and let him strengthen our resolutions with God's love, we might be strong enough to resist temptation or at least leave enough chocolate cake to share.

"There's only one power in the world great enough to help us rise above the difficult things we face: the power of God."
—Stormie Omartian

When You're Jealous

For where you have envy and selfish ambition,
there you find disorder and every evil practice.
—James 3:16

In the early 1960s, I sat on my bed at the Salt Lake City Crippled Children's Hospital, watching my wardmate, Sarah, chat with her folks. Sunshine poured into the third-story windows, glinting off the wheelchairs, as Sunday visiting hours began. Sarah's parents talked and laughed together. My nine-year-old heart turned green with jealousy.

Or was it envy? I not only wished I had a visitor, but I didn't want Sarah or any of the other patients to have visitors, either. I crossed my arms and stared at my striped bedspread as self-pity and loneliness blended with neon green jealousy and envy.

The other eleven girls on the ward knew the rules: stay on your bed from two until four-thirty, whether you have a visitor or not. We were supposed to read or do some other quiet activity so the lucky ducks could visit.

My parents lived two states away. I'd been at the hospital for nearly three months without a single visitor. Mom sent typed letters every week, but my heart ached deeply on Sundays. When the twin dragons of envy and selfishness breathed fire, I felt entitled to a bad attitude.

I wish I could say I outgrew such petty jealousy. But when I became the mom of four children, there was never enough of anything. Under peer pressure to provide for our kids, jealousy colored my relationships. Friends, relatives, and celebrities had what I needed or thought I needed. I prayed for God's provision but still ground the ax when others got a better deal.

I prayed harder. Surely God would see how much I deserved what I desired. But the more I sought God's special favor, the deeper jealousy and envy rooted in me.

If I coveted what others had, it only set me apart from them. Worse, coveting made me tightfisted about what I did have. Freely giving as Jesus modeled connects, enriches, and replaces jealousy with love.

I learned that jealousy is like a warning sign. When I feel like God gives others what I think should be mine, that warning sign flashes green. If I don't stop wanting what others have, my heart withers like a parched garden.

God began to show me the antidote to poisonous jealousy or envy. I finally understood that the path out of jealousy lies in giving. Forgiveness, thanksgiving, and generosity help me focus on what *others* need.

Giving time, resources, or love slays that green dragon. That long-ago Sunday, Sarah's mom came to my bedside and held my hand, making me feel loved. My heart sang while selfishness melted away. Jealousy is no match for love.

"Jealousy, that dragon which slays love under the pretense of keeping it alive."

— Havelock Ellis

When You're Restless

My soul is in deep anguish. How long, Lord, how long?
—Psalm 6:3

When my children were small, they measured time in terms of "sleeps." Whenever they were excited for something coming up, such as Christmas morning or a summer vacation, they asked every day. How much longer?

No matter how many more sleeps until the big day, to them, the wait seemed like forever. Anxiety and restlessness built so on the eve of whatever they awaited, all four of them practically bounced off the ceiling.

Most parents understand fidgeting, and restlessness often accompanies a child's expectations. By adulthood, most of us have learned coping mechanisms to keep ourselves calm no matter how many *sleeps* we must wait. Yet inside, we're a buzzy mess of *hurry up.*

We may know better than to harass God like our children might, asking the same question again and again. If we're truthful, we also admit how restless we feel.

I know these restless feelings well. After I'd earned my teaching certificate in Art Education, few districts were hiring new teachers. I prayed and waited or at least tried to wait. I told myself that God's timing is perfect, patience was a virtue, and a thousand years is like a day to God (2 Peter 3:8).

Waiting for a job offer definitely felt like a thousand years.

But then I noticed something. The more I dwelled on the waiting part, whether I prayed for a job or that my car wouldn't run out of gas again, the less I paid attention to the substitute teaching I was doing to make ends meet.

My distraction came to a climax one Friday as I subbed for a high school English class. Lunch had just ended, and the room was warm and stuffy. Plus, it was nearly the end of the school year. Like the students, I couldn't wait to get the class period over with, especially as I had an interview for a permanent position that afternoon.

My thoughts bounced from what to wear to what to say in my interview. My insides clutched with the same anticipation my children had experienced. All I had to do was get through this English class. I could barely stay still.

As I helped a student diagram a sentence, someone called out, "Can we go now?"

I glanced at the clock. Yes, the period was supposed to end right then. But I'd never taught at this school before and hadn't heard a dismissal bell. Maybe teachers had to release pupils themselves?

As they filed out, students snickered. While I daydreamed about my dream job, two boys had reset the clock's hands.

That day, the lesson for me was to focus on what God sets before me. I did get the job, but I had to stay present. I learned that if I give my full attention to the task at hand, God will carry me through as many sleeps as it takes.

"Patience is not the ability to wait, but the ability to keep a good attitude while waiting,"

—Joyce Meyer

When You're Big Mad

Refrain from anger and turn from wrath;
do not fret—it leads only to evil.
—Psalm 37:8

I've said it a thousand times. "You make me mad!"

Trouble is, that statement isn't true. We're in charge of our emotions, not other people or situations. Does that always keep me from letting anger erupt?

Not hardly.

Whether frustrated by work, parenting, politics, or my own choices, anger is a basic human emotion. God seems to have installed the mad button in all of us. Throughout the Old Testament, God displays anger against those who defy commands, rebel, or otherwise disobey God's directives.

And when God gets into wrath, look out. But careful reading uncovers what God really desires—a close relationship built upon mercy, justice, and forgiveness. These lead to love as modeled by Jesus.

I'm not quick to anger, but I've had a few Big Mad episodes. If I think a weaker person has been taken advantage of, my anger switch trips. Like the time I was a nine-year-old patient in a 1960s Children's Hospital. The girl in the next bed on the ward was older than I was, about fourteen. But cerebral palsy and developmental delays left her unable to walk and with the mind of a kindergartener.

One day, the nurse's aides came to her bedside and began berating her for soiling her bed. The aides yanked off her wet clothes and sheets without providing a screen for privacy, all the while telling her she was bad. I thought anyone, including God, would be Big Mad at the way she was treated. I piped up and told the aides to stop being mean to the girl. I got punished, but I didn't care. Anger was called for to advocate for someone who literally couldn't stand up for herself.

Only a week later, a few girls on the hospital ward started a club and didn't invite me to join. I was angry and so jealous that I bit the club leader on her arm. That time, God didn't seem to be happy with my behavior. I needed to learn that anger is a potent tool that must be controlled.

Be angry but do not sin (Ephesians 3:26) must be one of the most difficult tightropes to walk. We're not to sleep on our mad feelings or allow jealousy or envy to justify them. Scripture cautions us that too much fretting or worry can fester into anger that crosses over into evil.

Disappointment, entitlement, self-righteousness, or indignation seem to funnel straight into anger. The more excuses I make for myself, the less I hear God's call to love.

The hard part is knowing when anger is justified and when it's not. The path to godly Big Mad lies in following Jesus wherever he leads.

"For every minute you remain angry, you give up sixty seconds of peace of mind."

—Ralph Waldo Emerson

When You're Tired

My soul is weary with sorrow; strengthen
me according to your word.
—Psalm 119:28

New parents understand what weariness feels like, with feeding and diaper changing every couple of hours for weeks on end. After having two sons, I thought I knew what being tired felt like.

Then I delivered surprise twins.

Somehow, the second baby wasn't detected until after my daughter was born. In addition to feeling shocked, I rejoiced and thanked God for the premature but healthy pair. I felt happy, but ready for a long nap. That nap wouldn't be in my future for years.

With two newborns to care for all night and two little boys to wrangle all day, *fatigue* didn't begin to describe how my body felt: A beach ball losing all its air. Sisyphus rolling that boulder uphill. Those dancing roadside signs after they're deflated. Days and nights ran together. I was too tired to care.

Some days, God lifted me on eagles' wings, but lots of times God had to drag me through what seemed like unending chores. I did silly sleep-deprived things like putting the milk jug in the oven and forgetting my purse at the grocery store. I walked into my share of walls, but I learned that some kinds of tiredness are just part of the job description. Others are self-induced.

I knew better than to drive a car while I was sleepy but didn't realize that sparkling floors or home-cooked dinners weren't necessary during this season. God's gift of strengthening me to care properly for two newborns and two youngsters wasn't the same as overdoing household chores that few people would care about.

The kids are grown now, but God's still teaching me the same lessons. Back then, in a sleepless haze, I'd removed the newborn twins' hospital bracelets. For a moment, I panicked that I'd never be able to tell them apart. God reminded me that they were boy-girl fraternal twins.

In our modern, fast-paced lives, it's easy to work too hard, for too long, even as our bodies tell us to rest. When we're dog-tired, God longs to swoop us up and carry us awhile, even as we drink in renewal. All we need to do is fall into God's loving arms.

These days, fatigue hits me in different ways. Post-Polio Syndrome, with its various aches and pains, warns me to pace myself. I still often do more than my body can stand. But whether I'm exhausted or drained or feel as if I could drop where I stand, God reminds me that I worried I'd never be able to tell boy-girl twins apart. I smile and sink back into those Everlasting Arms.

"Sometimes the most productive thing you can do is rest and let your soul catch up."

—Anonymous

When You're Sick

Just then a woman who had been subject to
bleeding for twelve years came up behind him
and touched the edge of his cloak.
—Matthew 9:20

Down with a miserable illness, I longed to touch the hem of Jesus' garment.

While God sometimes works healing miracles, most of the time, I moan from my bed. As I suffer, whether from Post-Polio Syndrome or a head cold, I pray for comfort.

As a polio survivor, I thought I knew what suffering was. Growing up, I had many health problems, surgeries, and therapies. I never considered myself crippled, but I prayed for Jesus to stay with me during operations or painful procedures.

After almost forty years of marriage, my husband had a heart attack. He lost kidney function and needed hemodialysis three times weekly. For ten years, I cared for him, feeling helpless as he suffered internal bleeding episodes, heart failure, and the grind of dialysis.

I prayed, he prayed, friends and family begged God to heal my husband. A tough Marine, he never complained about each session's nearly four-hour procedure, or the risks if something went wrong.

At the dialysis center, so many patients endured a treatment that literally kept them alive. I prayed for them until I heard that small still voice urge me to do more.

I thought back to my wishes to touch the hem of Jesus' cloak in hopes of a miracle. What if, I seemed to hear, your experiences with disability and your husband's illness were training you to comfort others?

Really, Lord? What could I give these folks? Had I ever sat in a dialysis chair for hours while a tall, complicated machine cleansed my blood? I could barely glance at the giant needles used to hook patients to the machine.

Sure, I sometimes struggled with my polio-paralyzed arm, but my suffering wasn't in the same league as these patients.

But God insisted.

I donned a mask and gloves. My husband looked bored, so I prayed silently that his session would go smoothly and time would pass quickly. I squeezed his hand and went to another chair in the row.

If the person was sleeping, I said a silent prayer and moved on. Where possible, I said hello, gave my name, and asked theirs. Many seemed glad to chat. I prayed for their comfort and continued effective treatment.

I knew my husband and the others would need continued dialysis treatment. But even if the kidneys still needed dialysis, I knew at least one miracle had occurred that day. I learned that the hem of Jesus' garment is woven of love. If only for a little while, I'd touched it myself.

"Although the world is full of suffering, it is also full of the overcoming of it."

—Helen Keller

When You're Sick and Tired

Give thanks to the Lord, for he is good;
his love endures forever.
—Psalm 107:1

I couldn't stand it a minute longer.

My son's years of drug use and mental illness literally made me sick. In fact, a treatment center counselor once stared at me and said, "Do you know how sick you are?"

The counselor labelled me as a co-dependent enabler. For him to get well, I had to detach. Doubtless, my friends were tired of hearing me complain while nothing changed. Sick and tired, I had to do something.

But I was a total failure at tough love. Friends said I should stop enabling and let him hit bottom.

I couldn't cut off my own child. I loved him deeply. He'd struggled with life since he was young. He wasn't violent, although he brought chaos into both our lives, chaos that seemed unending. I felt stuck.

Well-meaning advice suggested I rid myself of the problem until my son straightened up and flew right. Yet I couldn't picture Jesus turning his back on sick persons when they made bad choices.

I could stay in that rut, putting up with chaos in the name of love. But we'd both simply become sicker and more tired. I figured I could only change myself.

Prayerfully, I set boundaries. I'd always thought boundaries were rules to show someone how you wanted *them* to act. Instead, good boundaries are for me and my well-being.

My values—to have a peaceful, loving home—dictated the boundaries. I wouldn't tolerate behavior that created chaos. The Golden Rule also reminded me to treat my son as Jesus would with unconditional positive regard.

In other words, I didn't have to accept behaviors that were threatening, disrespectful, or dangerous. I also needed to see my son not as his problems but as a child created in God's image and worthy of love.

These changes took time, lots of flubbing and realigning my goals. With Christ as my beacon, I could catch my son doing good, however small. I stopped grimacing when I spoke to him. I didn't disdain him for not doing what I wanted him to do. I no longer viewed him as a failure.

Gradually, my health improved. I'm no longer the doormat enabler. But I'm still a loving mom to this wayward grown child. Though it's hard at times, I can relate to him without despairing that sobriety will never come.

Today, instead of being sick and tired, we are building trust. God's love has a giant presence. My son is getting help with his problems. Of course, life isn't perfect. We're pretty human after all. But the opposite of addiction isn't just abstinence, it's connection. I'll never be sick and tired of my connection with my son.

"It always seems impossible until it's done."
—Nelson Mandela

When You Regret Choices

. . . he refreshes my soul. He guides me along
the right paths for his name's sake.
—Psalm 23:3

An elderly lady in front of me in the grocery checkout lane counted pennies.

I groaned inwardly. I'd chosen the wrong line. Again.

What seemed like a simple choice now felt so wrong. I might be a few minutes late for my next errand. Poor me. I had to step back and pray for a better attitude.

Today, everywhere we look, we face a million choices. From fifty brands of cereal to which checkout lane to stand in, we're bombarded. Thousands of cable channels, careers, and activities vie for our attention, all screaming, "Pick me!"

With so many choices, we're bound to regret some.

I doubt God cares if I choose the head of broccoli or a box of strawberries. And I always laugh at myself when I ask God for a parking spot. But some choices are more important—and I've had my share of regrets.

How can I cope with choices I wish I hadn't made?

A friend used to mix two adages about buttering bread and making one's bed: You buttered your bread, now lie in it. As funny as that is, the message is that we must learn to live with our choices, no matter how ill-advised. But is this what God says?

Scripture admits marriage can be a risky choice, and Saint Paul advises against it. But Paul also acknowledges that people do get married, and he gives guidelines that point to love. In I Corinthians 13:4-8, Paul gives a list of love's attributes. Love is patient, kind, does not envy or boast, is not proud, does not dishonor others, is not self-seeking, is not easily angered, and does not keep a record of wrongs. Love does not delight in evil but rejoices with the truth, protects, trusts, hopes, and perseveres. Love never fails (1 Corinthians 13).

If I make relationship choices according to those qualities, I should be very careful about tossing away those choices. We're cautioned against abandoning someone because the grass is greener or the person isn't perfect. The test for any relationship should be whether each partner demonstrates those love qualities.

Yet real life often collides with these ideals. We tend to make consequential choices such as education, career, and relationships when we're young—before wisdom has a chance to gain footing. If you're in an abusive relationship, safety and prayerful guidance trump perseverance. God desires life-giving choices such as health and well-being.

And love. Choices always come back to loving as Jesus loved.

The elderly woman in front of me slowly removed one coin after another from her purse. But something changed. God's love guided me to pray for her. I offered to carry her bag of groceries, and her smile lit my day.

When I picked the wrong grocery checkout line, I regretted my choice, but God had other plans.

"I'd rather regret the things I've done than the things I haven't done."

—Lucille Ball

When You've Hurt Someone

The tongue also is a fire, a world of evil among the parts of the body. It corrupts the whole body, sets the whole course of one's life on fire, and is itself set on fire by hell.
—James 3:6

At a funeral reception for my sister's brother-in-law, I managed polite chit-chat. The sister went on about overweight people. They just needed more willpower.

Nearly forty, I needed to drop some pounds left over from my pregnancy with the twins. "I can hardly see you if you stand sideways," I blurted out, "I'd hate to be that thin."

She looked crestfallen. Tears shone in her eyes before she turned away.

Once again, I'd hurt someone with my words.

People tell me I'm often funny. But when I speak first and repent later, people get hurt. In my world, too many people get poison dart treatment before I've thought things through.

The woman at that funeral didn't speak to me again for a while. Too late, I learned she has a condition that keeps her looking like a starved animal. She's self-conscious, while at the same time passing judgment on beefy girls like me. She didn't see my point of view. But I could have listened to the small still voice telling me to shut my pie hole.

To her, staying trim seemed simple: cut calorie consumption by keeping one's mouth shut, do not chew, or swallow. For me, (post-childbirth and run-ragged mom of two rambunctious boys and two infants who rarely slept), food was the only thing that kept me going.

Sometimes we aim our vitriol straight at another's heart. If you had a critical parent growing up, you know how words can build up or tear down.

Fear and judgment are major drivers of the fiery tongue mentioned in the Book of James. We fear what we don't understand, and we judge that which seems different from us. Both postures lead to *othering*. *Othering* hurts the targeted person or group.

As I walk with Jesus, I work to put aside the ways I tend to *other*. Each time I open my mouth to criticize or judge, I operate from fear. Perfect love (Christ) casts out fear (I John 4:18). By asking myself if my comment is kind and necessary, I stay closer to God.

When I mess up the way I did at that funeral, God gives grace to ask forgiveness. At another family gathering, I spotted the same relative. She was thinner than ever, her face gaunt. I approached anxiously, praying for the right words.

"You look lovely," I said. "You always do." I held my breath in case she said I was still too plump.

But God was in charge. She hugged me and whispered. "You always look great, too."

"It's not a person's mistakes that define them. It's the way they make amends."
—Freya North

When You Hurt

Night pierces my bones; my gnawing pains never rest.
—Job 30:17

Because of my physical disability from childhood polio, I've lived with muscle pain most of my life. Still, I'm not any better at coping with pain and hurt than most people.

Whether we hurt from physical or emotional pain, it's hard to get through life. When we hurt, we just want the pain to stop. But I read something long ago that opened my eyes to suffering. The advice was not to run from pain, but to stand in the middle of it.

How? When we reach our limit, how can anyone stand in the middle of the pain? The Pain Chart at your doctor's office rates pain from one to ten. What about the kind that's a zillion on that scale?

We tame chronic physical pain with analgesics. Pop a pill—over-the-counter or stronger, and the window of relief cracks open. But that window slams shut again after only minutes or hours. We must return again and again to that well of pharmaceuticals, mindful that the strong stuff risks dependency.

Some diseases rob us of basic abilities. My friend ended her life due to the fatal and progressive condition of ALS. When she could no longer swallow, she couldn't bear the hurt any longer.

Emotional hurt never gives a respite, and it can literally kill people with psychic suffering. The loved one's death, the awful diagnosis, the failing marriage, personal betrayals—these and more pile on until, along with clinical mental illness, pain reaches a zenith. Sadly, some people choose the way out that causes those left behind more hurt, more loss.

How can anyone stand in the middle of such agony?

No one can, on his own. That's why I call on Jesus every day to carry me through the things that hurt. Jesus doesn't mind swooping us up anytime we're exhausted by pain. He gives comfort and rest when we're desperate to feel better.

Notice, though, that Jesus doesn't often lift us out of hurt or snap fingers and make the discomfort go away. As much as I'd love a miracle or two, most of the time the Lord doesn't hand me one. Instead, God promises to walk through the valley of the shadow with us—loving us, comforting us, healing our hearts with love.

Even the paralytic who'd lain on his mat for thirty-eight years wasn't magically healed. Jesus asked, "Do you want to get well?" Then He commanded the man to stand up. Sometimes we get stuck in our brokenness. We sometimes need Jesus to not only carry us, but to shake us out of our suffering by saying, "Stand up!"

The real miracle is the way Jesus lovingly rushes in to stand in the middle of my pain, your pain, the hurting world's pain.

"The wound is the place where the light enters you."
—Rumi

When You Want to Get Even

Do not take revenge, my dear friends, but leave room for God's wrath, for it is written: "It is mine to avenge; I will repay," says the Lord.
—Romans 12:19

At my Worker's Compensation hearing, I was angry. My coworkers lied under oath. They told the judge that I was taking advantage of my disability by resting on the floor of the break room. That my back injury wasn't real. They mocked my testimony of having to crawl from the toilet because it hurt too much. I was devastated.

And a piece of me wanted to get even.

I scrawled a note to my attorney, but she didn't react. All I could do was deny the allegations and hope for the best. Secretly, I wanted a piano to fall on their heads from a third-story window. Or something that would prove I was right.

Eventually, I won the case and had to promise never to work for the organization again. But those lies still stung. And I admit that I'd be happy if something negative befell each person who wasn't truthful.

So often when we feel wronged, we not only want justice, but we want revenge. When others violate us in some way—whether it's robbery at gunpoint or cutting ahead in line—we boil with a thirst to even the score. Revenge is powerful enough to blind us from God's perspective.

Some people say they feel satisfaction when they take revenge. I've felt that way at times. However, a closer examination reveals that hurting others because they hurt me doesn't make things better. Accountability is important, but my sharpened sense of getting even extends beyond justice.

Revenge slingshots the seeker to a barbaric past, where an eye for an eye surpassed any chance for reconciliation or love. When I give in to hate or revenge or even envy (the feeling that I don't have something you have, but I don't want you to have it either), love doesn't stand a chance.

In that hearing room, love took a back seat as I clenched my teeth and silently fumed. I couldn't understand or accept why my coworkers chose to say untrue things about me that day. I felt that they never liked me and were now able to hurt me.

But what if they feared losing their jobs if they were honest? What if they didn't understand why my post-polio syndrome caused pain and debilitating fatigue? From their perspective, I must have seemed odd, bringing a yoga mat to recline on since the break room had nothing but metal folding chairs. Maybe they wished they could lie down for a midday rest, too.

I'll probably never know their reasons for saying inaccurate things that day. But I've let go of my need to get even. God wants to be the one to repay—and his mercies most often repay in love.

"Living well is the best revenge."
—George Herbert

When You're Pressured

Consider it pure joy, my brothers and sisters,
whenever you face trials of many kinds.
—James 1:2

Trying to pray, I kept my eyes shut.

But my young son broke in. "Mom," he said, "I can't find my other shoe."

I groaned and wished my eye would stop twitching.

For me, raising four kids was stressful. Two of my four were twins, born prematurely. The two older boys were in school. I had little time to catch my breath.

I was head chauffeur, chef, and maid. I thought I had to be a Proverbs 31 wife, and doer of everything.

But I was under too much pressure. My left eye twitched a lot, and although I had a short morning meditation time, I was snappish.

The cure for my stressful super-mom's life was to lessen the pressure. But how?

My family didn't see a reason to change. Children have needs, including locating missing shoes. My husband's busy work schedule often took him out of town. Even if he hadn't been the traditional breadwinner type, he literally wasn't there much to help.

I prayed about ways to lessen the pressure. To my surprise, all the suggestions were about changing myself.

For starters, I could delegate and lower my standards while the kids were little. I could stop saying yes to every request and be sure I could accept one without that frustrating eye twitch. And when I carved out my morning prayer time, was I being reasonable?

Most importantly, was I willing to let God carry me through this stressful phase? Could I be open to receiving Jesus' peace?

Over the next few weeks, I worked on getting organized. Instead of a haphazard schedule, I used a planner. I pulled back on volunteering and cut my work hours to part-time.

Things didn't always go smoothly. There were still emergency projects to finish before the next school day, and babies who upchucked on their outfits and mine five minutes before church. Life was *life*, with pressure and stress and last-minute calamities.

Gradually, my eye tic calmed. I made an area reserved for backpacks and books, along with a shoe rack. I planned meals and used a calendar. I met with God before the kids were awake.

Some life stresses can't be avoided or even foreseen. But our expectations don't need perfection. We can forgive ourselves if we aren't the best at some things and take steps to organize so we're ready when stuff goes awry.

When my child asked about his missing sneaker, I learned another important lesson. If Mom is deep in prayer, or if lunches aren't made and dust bunnies roam the floors like tumbleweeds, a loving answer turns away not just wrath but stubborn eye twitches, too. Stress melted as I took his hand, and we searched for the lost shoe.

"We can easily manage if we will only take, each day, the burden appointed to it. But the load will be too heavy for us if we carry yesterday's burden over again today and then add the burden of the morrow before we are required to bear it."

—John Newton

When You Mess Up

But who can discern their own errors?
Forgive my hidden faults.
—Psalm 19:6

Livid, my grown son glowered at me. "I can't believe you told him! I said that confidentially, not so you could spread it around the family."

I apologized, but he still seemed upset. For the next day, all I heard inside my head was, *You really messed up.* A familiar feeling of shame and guilt washed over me. I hadn't intended to gossip, but that's what it was. Talking behind someone's back, even if it is a family member, is passive-aggressive at best.

My son felt betrayed. He hadn't said, "don't tell this to anyone," but he trusted me to hold his confidence. I didn't realize that he wanted the information I'd shared kept between us. I avoided eye contact with him for a while, avoiding seeing him frown at me.

I doubt I'm the only person who's ever committed that kind of faux pas. Who hasn't let a secret slip out or misspoken in some way? We have a thousand ways to mess up, whether intentional or accidental. Small mistakes, like showing up for an appointment late or on the wrong day, can be fixed. But major things, like getting pulled over for a driving infraction or deliberately lying to someone who trusts you, seem harder to make right.

Most of us understand that to be good citizens, we follow laws and social mores. Though we do try to follow God's commandments, God knows we're going to mess up. That's why God encourages us to confess our sins or mistakes. Yet it's easy to become blind to our little mess-ups. After all, we don't rob or kill people or break the big commandments.

Jesus wants our personal relationships to be built on love, not blind obedience. " Jesus replied: 'Love the Lord your God with all your heart and with all your soul and with all your mind.' And the second is like it: 'Love your neighbor as yourself,'" Matthew: 22:36-39. The Lord wished for us to live in community with God and with each other.

When we do mess up (and we will), Jesus asks us to make it right with whomever we've wronged. An apology may or may not be accepted, but it's important to try to make amends for our own heart's sake.

Holding grudges or becoming bitter hurts me far more than others. If I mess up because my heart harbors darkness, I'm not able to access the full, abundant life God offers each of us.

Later that day, my son came and put his arm around me. "Sorry, Mom. I kind of overreacted. I love you."

It was the best thing I'd heard all day.

"We learn from failure, not success."
—Bram Stoker

When You're Heartbroken

He heals the brokenhearted and binds up their wounds.
—Psalm 147:3

For years, I'd watched my three precious sons suffer from mental illness and substance use. For a mom, nothing seems worse than seeing her children struggle. My heart broke again and again.

For years, I pleaded with God to make them well.

For decades, we sought out counselors, psychologists, doctors, and treatment centers. There were legal wrangles and job losses. Yet the guys still had problems.

Then I met a woman whose husband and three-year-old son had died after being swept out to sea on the Oregon coast. She'd watched helplessly as the ocean swallowed the ones she loved. Her loved ones were gone in an instant. We hugged and prayed long and hard.

My sons were dying too, except little by little, day by day.

We tend to judge heartbreak by the amount of severity suffered. Our society judges adversity by whether it's perceived to be random or self-induced. Drowning, or cancer, or a car crash feels random. Mental illness or substance use is still condemned as a choice.

Choice or not, heartbreak comes for all of us at one time or another. And when our hearts are torn in two, expectations are often at the root of the split. We envision a certain result, that our kids grow up and fledge as successful adults, and what we hope for comes to pass.

But when preferred outcomes aren't met, disappointment can fester into real suffering. They say people can actually die from a broken heart. Those who survive a wounded heart, often can't seem to find happiness again. The Scriptures tell us that "joy comes in the morning," But what if morning never comes?

God doesn't want us to be without hope but we can revive hope by entering into someone else's suffering. Walk a mile in their shoes. And maybe that's a key point. Experiencing hardship can prepare us to become more compassionate and console those whose hearts are broken.

When you're heartbroken, look for others who are heartbroken too. Weep together, help hold each other, remind yourself that Jesus can carry you both through this, too. In surrendering your broken heart to God, you may even discover a joy you didn't think possible.

I don't like the pain of heartbreak any more than anyone else. But I've suffered various trials and enough terrible stuff to recognize suffering when I see it. My experience with my sons propels me to help others who grieve over their children. Whether I'm a mom who's disappointed that her sons battle mental disorders and substance use or a mom who saw her son snatched away forever by a sneaker wave, love is the answer. Love and compassion for someone else's suffering may even lead to a heart that's bigger, not broken.

"What if joy, instead of a relief from heartbreak is what effloresces from us as we help each other carry our heartbreaks?"

—Ross Gay

When You Lose Someone Special

I give them eternal life, and they shall never perish;
no one will snatch them out of my hand.
—John 10:28

Mom was eighty-nine when she passed away. She had some dementia and could barely walk, her feet so crippled with infections that wouldn't heal. Those last few weeks, she stopped showering and ate little. She wanted to sing old hymns. She wanted to pray the twenty-third psalm—her favorite.

She knew God was calling her home.

In hospice, she kept calling for someone to get the boat. We laughed since our dad had raced boats in his younger days. Later, we learned that those in transition often speak of transport, as if they know they're going somewhere soon.

Many people struggle with what to say when a loved one is lost. "A better place" sounds comforting, but when others said it to me, I felt emptier than ever. People tried to console me, but the comment made me miss Mom even more.

Losing a loved one hurts. Although Christians reminded me that Mom was "with Jesus now," I felt as if someone stole the prize and I was left holding the empty paper bag.

Mom's heart was finally free of worry, anxiety, and guilt. Forever, she'd be with the Savior. She'd be reunited with our boat-racing father, the love of her life. I knew all that.

My heart, however, was in terrible shape. I had that ache that runs deeper than words, the raw pain of the empty place she once filled. Sure, I'd see her and all my loved ones eventually, but what about today?

I was a mess.

All I could do was to beg Jesus to carry me through this agonizing loss. And as I watched to be sure there was only one set of footprints in the sand, I was able to forgive trite or insensitive remarks.

No one really knows what eternal life is like. But if God is love, then love can never pass away. I may join Mom at the pearly gates. The afterlife may be beyond human comprehension. Yet love will sustain us on earth and in heaven. Jesus rose from the dead to help us make our way to the one true source of love. Then we can live forever with God, the Lamb, the Holy Spirit, and love itself. That's the only kind of reassurance that doesn't make me feel alone.

After Mom was gone, I went to her apartment to clean. There, on a table, I found a grocery pad with the entire twenty-third psalm written in her beautiful script. She knew where she was headed, all right. And that gives me great comfort as I grieve her loss.

"The song is ended, but the memory lingers on."
—Irving Berlin

When Life is God-Awful

He brought me out into a spacious place; he rescued me because he delighted in me.
—Psalm 18:19

I was lost.

In the San Diego hills, I drove to a women's Bible study with my two-and-a-half-year-old son and his newborn brother. Canyon gravel roads twisted and turned, and the street signs were confusing.

I made another wrong turn and tried to turn around, but my car's front tires slipped over the canyon's edge. The old Volvo teetered there. As a postpartum mom about to lose my mind, I couldn't pray fast enough or hard enough.

I've lived through my share of terrible days. So have you. Whether it's a morning gone wrong, a flat on the freeway, or the tragic loss of a loved one, everyone can point to a time where life seemed awful.

When your children are in danger, panic rises even faster.

I tried rocking the wheels but had no luck. Then, the Volvo shifted downward. I had to act.

In a crisis, every breath is a prayer, every thought an SOS. "Abba! Father!" I may have added, "Please get me outta here!"

When the situation isn't an emergency, I often become impatient. If I lose my keys, I pray but retrace my steps. If I'm disappointed by crummy news, I feel rejected, as if God wasn't paying attention.

And if an event lights my anger button, too often I speak before I think. My fiery tongue makes assumptions before I know the facts or consider anyone's feelings except mine. I usually have to apologize for my selfishness, callousness, or prejudice.

When we get hit with a no-good, awful event, if we react with our own wants or needs in mind, it means we're human. But God asks us to call upon him in troubles great and small. By letting love carry us through good days and bad ones, we can learn to see the ways God helps us and wants us to live life abundantly.

As I sat in that Volvo, a thought came. *Get the babies out safely.* I set the emergency brake, and the three of us went in search of help. At the first house I came to, a tall man in a cowboy hat answered. He was able to gun the car back up to the road. I thanked him, and we finally arrived at the Bible study.

When I told the story, a woman gasped. She said the man who helped me had died a year ago. I thanked God for sending angels to my rescue.

"Grow through what you go through."
—Eric Butterworth

When You Need a Breather

Yes, my soul, find rest in God; my hope comes from him.
—Psalm 62:5

The Saturday matinee ended, and I kept thinking about the Lone Ranger. I was nine or ten, and Mom had dropped me off at the movies by myself for the first time. I stood outside in the Yuma, Arizona heat, scanning the traffic for our family car.

Kids piled into idling cars, laughing and chattering about the triumphs of the masked hero. The crowd thinned, and soon I stood alone, trying not to cry. Where was Mom?

These days, we rush around, busier than ever. That day at the movies, there were no cell phones. I had no way to call my mother. Yet even today, I'm liable to forget important obligations. That's when I know I need a rest.

Raising my four kiddoes, I rarely had a moment to myself. I over-scheduled my days until I became physically sick. Migraines, eye twitches, or stomach issues alerted me to slow down and recharge my batteries.

I still experience times when life is hectic. Saying yes too often, I set myself up for failure, exhaustion, and illness. I may not be able to book a cruise or vacation in Europe, but thankfully, God has great ways to take a breather.

Jesus often told parables, but about rest, he was direct. "Come to me," Jesus instructed, "all you who are weary and heavy-laden, and I will give you rest," Matthew 11;28. The Lord doesn't specify that heavy-laden could mean an overstuffed planner and endless to-do lists. But anyone who can't handle one more thing knows the meaning of weary.

One of the beautiful truths about coming to Jesus is that he's always available, anytime and anywhere. Susannah Wesley, with a passel of young 'uns, would cover her face with her apron to signal she was in prayer. Her brief apron-over-the-head routine told the kids *don't bother me* in no uncertain terms.

These days, to enter Jesus' rest, we might need to turn off the phone or lock the bathroom door to find peace. When parents nourish their own souls, they are better equipped to lovingly guide their children. We can look forward to a peaceful respite if we allow ourselves to fall into the Everlasting arms.

As that girl waiting at the movie theater, I felt afraid my mother would never arrive. I prayed, and a few moments later, she pulled to the curb. She apologized for being late. Exhausted from working a full-time job, she'd fallen asleep. Whenever I'm weary and heavy-laden, I try to remember that, like Mom, I often need a breather and the peace only Jesus can give.

"When you rest, you catch your breath and it holds you up, like water wings . . ."

—Anne Lamott

When You're Not Enough

Hear my cry for mercy as I call to you for help, as I lift up my hands toward your Most Holy Place.
—Psalm 28:2

My parents always told me I was lucky. So lucky, they said, that polio only paralyzed one of my arms when I was eight and a half months old. Lucky that I wasn't in an iron lung or on crutches. So lucky.

How could I admit that I didn't feel lucky? My physical deficiencies screamed that I wasn't normal. Even worse, I was not enough.

I put on a brave face for the world. During my childhood, I underwent months in a hospital in another state, separated from my family while I underwent surgeries designed to help my arm and hand function better.

Those hospital stays taught me not to cry or complain, but inside, I felt terrified, pleading for help. The difference between my smiling face and my inner turmoil convinced me that I wasn't brave. I wasn't the overcomer I had to be.

Perhaps if those surgeries had been more successful, I might have been more thankful. But from my ten-year-old perspective, those procedures merely caused a lot of pain and loneliness. Each absence and recovery broadcast my disability to my classmates.

Until I had kids of my own, I thought I came by my assessments honestly. Then my four children had their own problems, their own feelings of not being enough. Slowly, my eyes opened to the fact that most of us feel inadequate at one time or another.

Maybe we're embarrassed that we aren't as successful in our career as we hoped. We think our nose is too big or our eyes are too small. We tend to focus on our flaws and think others sail through life with no problems. We enlarge our every shortcoming and mistake while seeing only the successful aspects in others. We worry that we're not enough.

Doubting oneself is common. But God never says we're failures. There may be areas that need improvement or significant change. But Jesus meets us where we are right now. We aren't required to change to be worthy of God's love.

God loves us so that we *can* change.

The more I embrace myself as *good enough,* the less I negatively judge myself. Our celebrity culture conditions us to believe that everybody should be an A-lister, with a perfect, toned body and money to burn.

Whenever I catch myself thinking I'm not enough, Jesus nudges me away from chasing human perfection. Love is God's standard of perfection. Disabled or not, nobody is *less than* in God's eyes. Better than luck, that's the power of love.

"No one can make you feel inferior without your consent."

—Eleanor Roosevelt

When You Can't Sleep

When you lie down, you will not be afraid; when
you lie down, your sleep will be sweet.
—Proverbs 3:24

When our twins were small, I read stories, sang to them, and tucked them into bed. In the morning, I often found both of them asleep in our bedroom. One bedded down on the cedar chest at the foot of the bed. The other curled up on the floor next to my side.

When I asked why they couldn't sleep in their own room, they said, "We were scared, Mommy. We couldn't sleep."

If I can't sleep, I sometimes wish I could sneak into God's bedroom. Most times, I have insomnia because my mind won't stop. My thoughts race in circles because I'm anxious about something. Fearful. Scared.

Sometimes I worry I might not meet a new challenge. Or I feel bad for saying something unkind. I regret passing up a chance to be kind to someone else. Those nights, my sleep anxiety grows heavier with every passing hour. I know, because I glance at the clock every five minutes.

Beyond pharmaceuticals or other aids, what can we do to get a decent night's sleep? Studies show that not sleeping for a long period can actually kill a person. Perhaps that's why torture often involves sleep deprivation. Insomniacs take medications, drink herbal teas, or rely on preferred methods to attain good sleep. Some use non-habit-forming over-the-counter medications or read books before bed.

For some, insomnia happens occasionally. Others deal with sleeplessness on a regular basis. Either way, the harder I try to drift off, the more awake I feel. Lying there, staring into the night, prayer is a great way to distract my buzzing mind. Repeating the Lord's Prayer, going through my prayer list, or counting my blessings helps get to dreamland.

Rest. Ah, to relax. To awake feeling refreshed and ready for the day sounds heavenly. And it is heavenly. Whether we imagine Jesus sitting beside us humming a lullaby or meditate on Scripture, we can let our busy thoughts lean back and relax. Breath prayers such as breathing in *love* and breathing out *Jesus* can pull us into the Savior's arms, arms that will gently rock us to sleep.

My twins finally outgrew their nightly forays into our room. But they knew safety and love waited for them in their parents' presence. When sleep eludes, Jesus can carry us away to dreamland. When deep sleep remains just outside reach, we can rest in the arms of love.

"I find the nights long, for I sleep but little and I think much."
—Charles Dickens

When You're Hanging by a Thread

So we say with confidence, "The Lord is my helper; I will not be afraid. What can mere mortals do to me?"
—Hebrews 13:6

Despite heart stents placed to open clogged arteries, my husband suddenly turned ashen gray.

I wasn't aware I'd been holding my breath. When I finally drew in a gulp of air, reality slammed my chest. Machines beeped. I yelled for the medical staff to help him. His face faded from pale gray to stark white. I didn't know if he'd make it. With God on speed dial, I prayed harder than I'd ever prayed.

The medical team rushed him back to surgery and replaced the stent that had failed. My hands, raw from trying to hang on to my faith, praised the Lord for pulling my brave ex-Marine back from the edge.

But days later, doctors couldn't figure out why he wasn't recovering. The poor guy couldn't eat, could hardly walk, and seemed so different. I was in charge of seeing to it that he took the many new meds. None seemed to help.

My husband wasn't old enough for a senior discount. Now, I faced the possibility that his breadwinner days were over. I gulped at the thought of living without him.

We loved each other and together had raised four children. We weren't a perfect couple—throughout our marriage, we struggled financially. I had stopped working due to my polio disability. Now I was desperate for God to save my husband.

What if we lost our home? How would I care for a disabled spouse? What if I ended up alone?

My future dangled like spider silk, waving in the wind.

After weeks of medical tests, doctors remained unsure of a diagnosis. He continued to get worse. I prayed harder, begging God for help.

One day I noticed strange purple marks around his waist. I took photos and showed them to the doctor. Those marks revealed the condition: cholesterol embolism. His kidneys were plugged permanently. He would need hemodialysis for the rest of his life. Thankfully, God saved his life and that was what mattered.

When life unravels, we tend to plead for miracles and instant answers. It can feel disappointing when God doesn't do what we think is best. Yet if we look closer, we see Jesus holding us up, carrying us no matter how awful the circumstances.

God's answer wasn't the miraculous one I'd hoped for. My husband needed dialysis for life, but he's live. Although there was no instant healing, God miraculously carried me through a frightfully tough time. My slender thread of faith had nearly broken, but God gave me strength to hang on.

"The only way around is through."
—Robert Frost

When You Need a Friend

You are my friends if you do what I command.
—John 15:14

I stood with my back against the wall. The faculty party echoed with chatter punctuated by laughter. I knew most of the teachers there, but I'd never felt so alone.

I scanned the room, searching for friends, but those in my department seemed deep in conversation. I pulled my sweater closer. Why did it feel so cold in here?

I'm not especially shy—my first dream was to become an actress. I taught my public-school art classes with ease and had no qualms about public speaking. Yet somehow, large gatherings reduced me to a wallflower. I was terrified to insert myself into a group of teachers and even more afraid of approaching strangers. I prayed for God's help and hoped I didn't look as lonely as I felt.

At that time, the WWJD bracelets were popular, and I wore one too. What would Jesus want me to do in a crowded room?

I'd been studying Paul's letter to the Galatians. A line of Scripture floated back to me: *You reap what you sow.*

At first, I was puzzled. Aside from holding up the wall, I hadn't sown much of anything at the party. Everyone seemed to be having a nice time. How did Paul's words apply to this setting?

I shifted my weight, wondering if I should slip out the side door. No one had spoken to me, so maybe leaving was best. I started toward the door, careful not to make eye contact with anyone.

And bumped straight into a teacher I'd never met. Rather short, with mouse-colored hair that fell across her eyes. Her name tag read, *Sue G., English Department.*

I mumbled, "Sorry," and kept walking. But then something my grandmother once said stopped me.

"To have a friend," Grammie had said, "you must be a friend."

I smiled, extended my hand, and introduced myself. Sue's eyes lit up, and she smiled back. We struck up a conversation, and I relaxed.

Jesus said to love our neighbor (Matthew 22:36-39). We can sow friendly cues that invite others to engage. Waiting for others to hold out a hand of friendship only lets us reap loneliness.

Making friends with Sue made the faculty party much more enjoyable. While those we invite to friendship don't always take us up on the offer, we can at least demonstrate our obedience to Jesus' command. Paul and my grandmother both knew the secret of friendship is being open to loving one's neighbors—all our neighbors. Many years later, Sue and I are still friends.

"Try to be a rainbow in someone's cloud."
—Maya Angelou

When It's a New Day

Because of the Lord's great love we are not consumed, for his compassions never fail. They are new every morning; great is your faithfulness.
—Lamentations 3:22-23

I couldn't sleep again. I'd tried warm milk, reading, and counting sheep. Nothing worked. As the clock ticked, my anxiety ratcheted up. Fear seized me. I felt an urgency to get up and walk around.

As late evening gave way to night, I told myself that I was being ridiculous. So what if I couldn't drift off as usual? I wouldn't die if I lost a little shuteye. But each time I lay down, the same fear rose until I jumped out of bed and walked.

I talked to a family member who was still awake. He recommended his over-the-counter sleep medicine. "How about a shoulder massage?" he asked.

By now it was past midnight. "No," I said. "I'll just keep trying."

I scooted to the other side of the bed—the side where my late husband had slept. No dice. I grabbed a pillow and went to the living room sofa. I propped myself on one end, leaning into the pillow. At least I could rest my eyes.

I remembered my own mother's long-term insomnia. Once when I was a teen, I tried to sneak in after curfew. There was Mom, ironing clothes at three in the morning. See, I told myself. Lots of people struggle with sleep.

But I simply couldn't get to dreamland, and it felt like life or death. I cried out to God. Help me, help me.

God's answer was to sing.

Mom had told me that she sang when she couldn't sleep. For me, running a song through my head was better than belting out *God Bless America* like she did. I played hymns in my mind as if I were a jukebox or a deejay. Old favorites such as *Be Thou My Vision* and newer praise songs rang out in my head. I even sang *Amazing Grace.*

I stayed awake a while longer, recalling favorites from worship and life. I stopped eyeing the clock and simply allowed myself to imagine singing at Jesus' feet. As I sang, the dust and cares from my life fell away. My heartbeat kept time with love itself.

Around the world, insomnia claims many victims. I'm sure at least some of them face a deep and irrational fear as they struggle to find rest. Maybe your singing voice is sublime, or maybe you can't carry a tune in a bucket. But if all else fails and you worry that the morning will never come, remember that Ephesians 5:19 says, "Sing and make music from your heart to the Lord." Similarly, Psalm 100:2 says, "Worship the Lord with gladness; come before him with joyful songs." Sing to Jesus and even if you don't fall asleep, you'll be filled with our Lord's comfort and compassion.

God promises that night won't last forever—there *will* be a new day. Lamentations 3:22-23 assures, "Because of the Lord's great love we are not consumed, for his compassions never fail. They are new every morning; great is your faithfulness." That's worth singing about—even in the middle of the night.

"In your darkest hour, give thanks, for in due time, the morning will come. And it will come with a ray of sunshine."

—Michael Bassey Johnson

When the Sun Comes Out

He will make your righteous reward shine like the dawn, your vindication like the noonday sun.
—Psalm 37:6

My eyes must have been as wide as saucers. "Sweetie," I said to my kindergartener standing outside our door. "What are you doing here?"

His blonde hair glinting in the morning sun, he stared at the ground and muttered, "I don't like my teacher."

I gathered him close. "Don't you want to go to school like big brother?"

He pulled away and started to cry. He wasn't going to return to his class willingly. I made a mental note to phone the school office. Again. My sunny little boy ran away from kindergarten every chance he got.

Scenes like that became common. He'd changed. He didn't only grow taller and master big-boy tasks like tying his shoes. His entire personality went from sunny to somber.

I blamed myself for giving birth to premature twins. To put it mildly, I was overwhelmed. The babies weren't just preemies. They were a total surprise. My middle son changed radically just after their birth. It convinced me that as I juggled two infants one-handedly, he was left out of the nurturing he needed.

My prayers for him were a mixed bag of urgent "please heal him" and "I-can't-deal-with-this." Many nights, I cried out in desperation, unsure of how to parent a special needs child.

As the years went by, he tried to adjust to school and home, church and friends. He was a leftie and artistic but refused to take off his jacket no matter what the room temperature. He repeated TV commercials over and over and disliked being hugged. As someone with an advanced degree in Learning Disabilities, I suspected autism. That diagnosis did nothing to help with his odd habits and social anxiety. By eighth grade, he was tutored one-on-one—the only way he'd attend school.

Unfortunately, he was often irritable and grumpy. Family outings became endurance tests. Even when we planned a fun activity, sometimes my husband and I couldn't even get him into the car. I felt helpless and hopeless. The only thing I did right was to keep praying for him.

Too many of us have loved ones who are difficult, addicted, mentally ill, or just cantankerous. All we can do is try to get through interactions with as loving an attitude as we can muster. So often I fail. Yet knowing that Jesus is there alongside to help with the heavy lifting and go through trying times gives courage to be there for my special needs child or challenging family members.

My son often still acts as if a dark cloud hovers above him. But now and then, he'll give me a quick hug or break into laughter. That's when the sun really comes out, and that's what gives me hope.

"Keep your face to the sun and you'll never see the shadows."

—Helen Keller

When Jesus Surprises

Jesus did not let him, but said, "Go home to your own people and tell them how much the Lord has done for you, and how he has had mercy on you."
—Mark 5:19

When I was nine years old, I spent months away from home at a hospital in a different state. Without family or friends nearby, I had major surgery on my paralyzed arm. I was terrified a lot of the time, both of the painful procedures and the loneliness.

I prayed, mostly to go home. Told I'd be in the hospital longer, I felt God had deserted me. Maybe God didn't even like me. A good God wouldn't leave me in a strange place for months without my mom visiting even once. Each night I gazed into the night, wondering why God wouldn't give me a miracle.

That's why, for years, I only believed the idea of Jesus. People around me gushed about how the Lord was their best friend, how that personal relationship with Jesus Christ had changed and transformed them. As the song said, he walked and talked with them.

I wanted all that, but for me, God felt dangerous. My church upbringing led me to think God was vindictive and often mean.

I tried to read my Bible. But even the red-letter words of Jesus bounced off me like a bunch of Nerf darts. When I tried to speak in tongues, my sister laughed and said I sounded like bad Chinese.

I wasn't a hypocrite, off sinning up a storm while claiming piety. I just didn't think of Jesus as a friend as much as someone who was always mildly disappointed in me. The people who taught me how to regard the creator concentrated on following rules and the punishments that happened to those who didn't fear God enough. I didn't understand how to grow a true intimate relationship. Jesus was a guy who had some great teaching but wasn't around when I needed him most.

As an adult, I viewed God as a kind of mean Santa Claus. I'd pray for an outcome, but if a miraculous sign didn't appear, I concluded that I was unworthy. That little girl in the hospital was still sure God didn't want to be her friend.

I doubt I'm alone in feeling as if God is often far away. That God is too busy or somehow not interested in granting miracles. But when we back God into a prayer corner, we often can't see that Jesus is right beside us. Loving, comforting, and abundantly dishing out compassion.

When I finally saw how much Jesus wants the abundant life for us, as in John 10:10, "The thief comes only to steal and kill and destroy; I have come that they may have life, and have it to the full," suddenly, he became real to me. Even if the miracle doesn't come, he sticks with me through it all. What a nice surprise.

In that hospital long ago, I felt scared and lonely. I kept my Bible under my pillow and stared into the night. Although I wasn't sure about Jesus, he was sure about me.

"Let's not be afraid to receive each day's surprise, whether it comes to us as sorrow or as joy."

—Henri Nouwen

part two

When You Want Out, He Carries You

When You Really Want Out, He Carries You Through

"Cast all your anxiety on him because he cares for you."
—1 Peter 5:7

I'm not brave. The horrors and atrocities some people endure—wrongful detentions, brutal beatings, and even death at the hands of oppressors make me look pretty lily-livered. I can't imagine being paralyzed from the neck down or tortured by unseen voices, or living through a raging fire, flood, tornado, or hurricane.

We don't always face natural disasters, or life-altering diseases, or disabilities. Our calamities can be as common as being rejected, losing a job, or having more month than money. Whenever trouble arrives, God wants us to run to our prayer closets, to look to the Source (Mathew 6:6). Yet we often try to pray away our greatest trials, begging for miracles rather than endurance. In our humanness, we want the pain—whether from tragedy or heartache or boredom—to end. Please, dear God. Now.

If God tends to pluck you out of every terrible situation as soon as it arises, I'm happy for you. That's wonderful. Personally, instant relief doesn't happen to me very often. That's why I need to remind myself that, whatever the horrible, God will walk through it with me. When we can't go on, Jesus will carry us through.

As I draw nearer to God, I'm starting to understand that a lack of miracles doesn't mean God's mad. Or that God's too busy or that God needs me to suffer. Jesus tells us that in this world we will have trouble (John 16:33). And what better companion than the Lord to go through the crud that life slings at us?

The picture of Jesus carrying me through the flames is hard to appreciate when I'm in the middle of trouble. Like a mother in the transition phase of labor, when the worst pain hits, I tend to curse and moan and want the pain to be over. When we're in the middle of something icky or sorrowful and start to doubt that we'll make it through, we can relax into Jesus' arms. It may not seem true in the midst of challenges right now, but Jesus promises to carry you through (Hebrews 13:5).

"God uses rescued people to rescue people."
—Christine Caine

When You're Living in Trauma

The hearts of the people cry out to the Lord. You walls of Daughter Zion, let your tears flow like a river day and night; give yourself no relief, your eyes no rest.
—Lamentations 2:18

She was my favorite aunt, like a mother but not as hypercritical. She listened to my teenage complaints in ways my own mom never did. She was pretty and adored dragonflies. I loved her so much.

She died only weeks after Mom's death. The two passings felt like being hit by semi-trucks loaded with boulders. Drowning in a pool of trauma, grief weighed me down like a millstone. I spent hours in the garden, trying to find goodness again. But I couldn't cry.

The loss continued. A treasured neighbor died much too young. A friend's thirty-something son overdosed. Another friend's young adult son was killed while riding a bicycle. Even my old cat had to be euthanized.

After eight deaths in a short amount of time, I walked around like a zombie in a flat, gray world. Depression seized me in ways I'd never experienced before. My husband still needed care as a thrice-weekly hemodialysis patient. I had other obligations too, including the urge to look strong for my family. Still, I begged God to tell me why my tears didn't come.

I thought that God carrying me meant I'd have an iron will—nobody would see me break down. Besides, weren't all these loved ones in a better place now? Why would I cry over that?

We often worry that others will see us still trudging through trauma and conclude that we're weak or self-pitying fools. But when trauma happens—a disaster, death, any kind of loss, it's easy to forget that we can live its painful side effects. Trauma hangs itself on our skins like lead aprons, leeching our strength even as God carries us.

But just as there's no timeline for grief, past trauma can inform everything we are today. We live the trauma albatross, carry PTSD around without remembering it's still hanging on our backs.

God's promise to carry us through whatever trauma we've experienced doesn't mean that Jesus makes small talk while we strain under the weight of our catastrophes (Isaiah 46:4).

No. God may not miraculously wave away all our traumas and troubles, but God definitely wants to help shoulder the burden. In Matthew 11:28, Jesus says, "Come to me, all you who are weary and burdened, and I will give you rest." *I'll spot you on lugging the baggage, lend a hand when the backpack straps dig deep into your flesh, grant you so much love that you'll either laugh or cry. Just come.*

When trauma sticks like a bad odor, it can feel impossible to find joy again. But this morning, as I sat in the garden, a blue dragonfly hovered over a blooming Iris. I thought of my favorite aunt and marveled at the way God had bundled me into the Everlasting Arms, carrying me from moment to moment. Without even noticing, tears slipped down my cheeks.

"Grief is the price we pay for love."
—Queen Elizabeth II

When You Sugarcoat Trauma

Finally, all of you, be like-minded, be sympathetic,
love one another, be compassionate and humble.
—I Peter 3:8

Whenever I was sent to the children's hospital in another state, Mom always reminded me to *look on the bright side.* My grandmother urged me to be brave and thankful for the surgeries and treatments I received there.

But at nine years old, I couldn't see a bright side to being torn away from family and friends for major orthopedic surgeries on my polio-paralyzed arm. I didn't feel brave or lucky. Only guilty and sad.

So guilty that I never complained to anyone. I put on a brave face and never confessed my fears or that a lot of really scary pain was involved in this *lucky* treatment.

Grammie and Mom both lived through the Great Depression and World War II. They, like many of those generations, used songs and sayings to stay hopeful. *Every cloud has a silver lining. Stay on the sunny side. Count your blessings.*

The hospital also demanded courage from patients. The place was institutionalized, and patients were expected to be brave. Anything less was punished. If a patient cried, a nurse might haul their bed down the hall for disturbing the others. Even though my parents never visited, I learned never to complain or cry during three-month stays.

Still, Mom sugarcoated my ordeal, promising a second Christmas or some grand vacation as a reward for my cooperation. Her letters were newsy and cheerful, which made me feel ashamed for feeling bad.

When we don't let anyone in on our pain, it simply compounds. If unhealed, we end up shouldering heavier burdens than the trauma itself. I'm sure Mom meant well, but at times I longed to melt into her arms and sob.

As a kid, I felt frustrated that God didn't give me the miracle of being released as soon as I wished. I doubt I'd have cared that my character was being molded by the challenge. I just wanted to go home.

When I finally returned, the sweet glossing-over continued. My family didn't want to hear about the pain of surgery or the loneliness that made me keep my white Bible under my pillow. To heal that sort of trauma, I needed to run to God who saw me trembling on the operating table and knew I cried at night into my pillow.

For years, I couldn't allow anyone to see my sorrow. But when I had my own family, I made sure the children knew they could come to me with broken hearts or bawling like a stray lamb.

That same God reaches out to you, to me, and to anyone who feels unheard or unseen. When Jesus carries us, he lets us bend his ear. He listens without glossing over our pain with old cliches or fake-happy sayings. Without sugarcoating those wounds we've kept quiet about for so long, Jesus carries our traumas, past or present.

"Save the sugarcoating for the donuts.
Honesty is what people want from you."
—Mel Robbins

When You're a Competitive Sufferer

The Lord is gracious and righteous; our
God is full of compassion.
—Psalm 116:5

On a cold winter day, weighed down by a cold, I blew my nose. Aunt May had dropped in to visit without calling ahead. I didn't really want company, but I apologized for my froggy voice. "This cold is giving me a headache."

Aunt May, tall with silky white hair, didn't miss a beat. "Oh," she rubbed her temples, "Lord knows *I've* had the worst migraine for days. My doctor thinks I clench my jaw while I sleep." She leaned closer. "But I'm sure it's something more serious."

I stifled a cough. "I'll pray for you."

She rolled her eyes. "Day before yesterday, I waited hours in the emergency room. All I got was pills and a mouth guard."

I smiled and hoped she didn't plan to stay long. No matter how sympathetic I was to her ailments, my aunt's conditions were always much worse than mine or anyone else's. I couldn't help thinking she was a competitive sufferer.

We've all known people who, for whatever reason, must top our achievements or calamities. If we say we're happy about something we're doing, this person has done bigger and better things. If we suffer any trauma, that same person has suffered more.

At one time, these folks irritated me to no end. Why did they insist on training the spotlight on themselves, no matter the circumstances? The one-ups were infuriating.

Listening to them whine or boast about their lives—while at the same time ignoring my feelings—felt disingenuous and tiring. I caught myself avoiding Aunt May and others like her. Sometimes, I didn't answer the door.

But God had other ideas. What I needed wasn't only someone to listen to me. I needed a softer heart, one that could appreciate how much my aunt was suffering. How much she craved attention, someone to care.

With God's help, instead of hiding, I considered why someone like Aunt May might resort to competitive suffering. She lived alone, and her children seldom visited.

We've all known people who tax our patience. Whose illnesses or traumas are always worse than ours. Stepping back from the competition, we might see scared and lonely people who need extra love.

As I viewed her more like Jesus might, I understood how easy it was to help her gain that reassurance she was desperate to receive.

"I'm afraid it's cancer," Aunt May whispered.

I took her hand. "Jesus knows for sure. Why don't we pray right now?"

Aunt May's shoulders relaxed, and she smiled.

"Be kind and merciful. Let no one ever come to you without coming away better and happier."

—Mother Teresa

When You Cling to Blindness

Now my eyes will be open and my ears attentive
to the prayers offered in this place.
—II Chronicles 7:15

For the last two years of his life, my beloved husband was practically blind. He'd worn eyeglasses most of his life, but toward the end, no prescription seemed right. He totaled two different vehicles and stashed magnifying lenses throughout our house. But he refused to admit that he couldn't see.

In other areas, the man I loved seemed to *choose* blindness. He'd had a very rough childhood. When he was five years old, his mother survived a car crash but sent him and his younger sister to a Catholic Mission while she recovered. Apparently, he won a roomful of expensive toys on a local kids' TV show, but the Mission took the toys away. He never got over that loss and afterward hoarded possessions.

Yet in adulthood, he refused to see that no one was going to take his stuff. His serious childhood trauma led him to be willfully blind about generosity and sharing. With severe post-traumatic stress disorder (PTSD) as a result of his tours of duty in the Vietnam War, he kept baseball bats or heavy pipes behind every door. He thought his actions were simply sensible, but his experience in the war made him hypervigilant.

I spotted my husband's willful blindness, but of course, I couldn't see the places that are painful to *me*. Bad experiences can do that. I deal with PTSD from my childhood hospitalizations but, to cope, we look past or refuse to see the ways blindness holds us back. A certain sound or smell can trigger horrible memories. We rush to protect ourselves, forgetting that God is right there with us.

Everyone deals with troubling events in their own way, and refusing to think or talk about them isn't necessarily bad. But when we separate ourselves from others, become angry, fearful, or stuff our feelings deep inside, we risk cutting off the love and understanding we might otherwise receive.

Visiting past trauma and refocusing our blind spots takes courage and determination, and sometimes, good therapy. Jesus tells people to pluck the log from their own eye instead of harping on their neighbors' splinter. He knows willful blindness prevents us from the freedom of God's love.

But if we remember that God carries us even through these hurtful past places, we can approach healing with a fresh eye toward love, forgiveness, and hope for tomorrow.

My wonderful Marine of a husband bore the weight of many traumas over his lifetime. His blindness, both physical and emotional, often held him back from enjoying life and recognizing God's presence, carrying him along. Every now and then, love broke through, and he'd rejoice. I like to think God's spectacles helped him see clearly, if only for a time.

"Only love has clear vision."
—Iris Murdoch

When You Can't Stand the Pain

How long, Lord? Will you forget me forever?
How long will you hide your face from me?
—Psalm 13:1

I held back Vivian's long red hair as she retched. In the sixties, there were no call buttons or phones in the children's hospital. We waited for a nurse to come by.

Vivian had cerebral palsy and couldn't walk. Talking was difficult. Her spastic muscles meant she couldn't use her hands either. I was glad to hold a barf pan for her when she was sick.

As a crippled kid in the children's hospital, I compared my disability to the other patients. Since I was almost always the only one who could walk unaided, I thought my problems were minuscule compared to others. Some girls were in plaster casts from waist to toes, while a few unlucky ones sweated inside full-body casts. And some were like Vivian.

I had one paralyzed arm and hand, wrapped in plaster and a bandage splint from my recent muscle transfer surgery. My fingers were swollen, purplish, and throbbed. I wasn't supposed to be out of bed, and nurses warned me to keep my arm above my heart. But Vivian couldn't help her sick stomach either.

Even worse, hours earlier, the poor girl had howled in pain as a doctor performed a lumbar puncture. Seemed more like torture to me. And upchucking wasn't pleasant either.

As I held the pan to Vivian's chin, the nurse on duty appeared. She scolded and I dove back into my bed, banging my splinted arm on the guardrail. Now *I* wanted to howl. Pain shot through and boomeranged from my fingers to my shoulder. The intense pain made me feel like throwing up, too.

In medical settings, we are asked to rate our pain from one to ten. While useful for rating physical pain, are those numbers just another way to compare ourselves? How can anyone rate a broken heart? Psychic and emotional pain often defy any one-to-ten scale. They can be far harder to endure, especially when that pain is carried alone.

God doesn't measure pain on a scale. Jesus opens his arms wide, no matter where or why we hurt. Your pain is real because it is yours. Even when others don't understand your suffering, God waits—ready to offer love and comfort—whether you whisper your need or cry out for help.

After I bonked my splint, I buried my face, trying not to cry or yell. I reached once again for the little white Bible under my pillow, desperate for relief, begging God for strength.

When I looked up, there was Vivian, smiling at me.

Her long red hair shining, she managed to say, "You're so strong."

To my surprise, I was.

"There are dark shadows on the earth, but its lights are stronger in the contrast."
—Charles Dickens

When You Let Go of Victimhood

Do everything without complaining and arguing
—Philippians 2:14 (NLT)

My creative writing student, Luther, always seemed to have an excuse.

His explanations were better than the dog eating his homework, but not much. Tall with dark, soulful eyes, he was talented and well-spoken, and his writing was intriguing and poetic. Yet he seemed to talk about writing more than actually producing stories.

Luther started short stories but left them unfinished. His fictional characters came alive in his scenes, only to fizzle and take the easy way out. He reminded me of a neighbor who often told me about situations in which she was the victim.

The first few times Cyndy complained about her life, I sympathized. She did seem to get the short end of life—the car company failed to repair her vehicle correctly. Her doctor hadn't prescribed the meds she knew were best. If something could go wrong, it did. And always in dramatic fashion.

Luther and Cyndy each irritated me with their parade of moaning and gripes. Businesses ripped them off. Doctors were quacks. Luther couldn't write because of an emergency. For all I knew, the emergency was that the sky was falling. After a while, I began to avoid them both.

I prayed for them halfheartedly until God posed a question. Where was I always a victim?

Maybe it was when I complained to another teacher about lazy students. Or when I had to bite my tongue to avoid telling Cyndy she was a drama queen. As I held the victim label to the light, I saw that even the Israelites wandering in the desert constantly murmured about all that God *hadn't* given them.

Instead of judging, God didn't scold me or tell me to quit being a victim. Jesus brought to my attention both Luther and Cyndy but stripped of my judgments. Luther might be holding down a demanding job or dealing with family crises. Cyndy could be coping with a failing marriage, a dying parent, or trauma from childhood. In Jesus' light, I could see real people battling their fears instead of shallow complainers who were always the victim.

My heart softened, but only after Jesus loved me into a place where I could see more clearly. Changing my judgmental nature was hard, but I began to see places where I could accept responsibility rather than harbor a victim mentality.

Seeing Luther and Cyndy through a lens of love made me so much more generous and tolerant. Even if others in my life don't get past victimhood, by leaning on God's love, I'm in the process of finding ways to appreciate the many gifts God gives us each day.

"A wise woman wishes to be no one's enemy; a wise woman refuses to be anyone's victim."
—Maya Angelou

When You See Other Viewpoints

Do not forget to show hospitality to strangers,
for by so doing some people have shown
hospitality to angels without knowing it.
—Hebrews 13:2

My adoptive grandfather disliked anyone who identified with a Christian denomination different from his.

As a girl of around ten, I asked my grandmother why Grandpa hated those people. She said he had been cheated by someone and therefore hated the entire lot.

I said, "But how could you hate people you'd never met?"

She changed the subject. I wasn't satisfied, but as I grew up, I understood that lots of folks disliked anybody who was different from them. When civil rights, desegregation, and women's rights roiled the nation, tensions ran high. People were beaten, and some died trying to claim their rights. I was just a kid, but I thought that God's love might be the answer to all the strife.

Maybe my views came from being a disabled child. I knew how much it hurt to be singled out or made to feel less than. As I studied my Sunday School Scripture reading schedule, I read over and over that Jesus loved people no matter what. In fact, Jesus seemed to like the lowliest and least the best of all. He told us the most important things we are to do: to love God and our neighbor (Matthew 22:37).

These days, we seem to be encouraged to choose sides more than ever. Whether you're rich or poor, athletic or disabled, a cat person or a dog person, we're pressured to be on the popular side of everything. With information and news at our fingertips twenty-four-seven, it's harder than ever to climb out of our comfort zone and meet people who may be very different in race, ethnic customs, career, or degrees of success or failure. Some people feel so desperate to measure up that they give up.

But God calls us to love. Jesus holds out his nail-scarred hands, entreating us to have compassion. If we have to lay down roots for a position, a belief system, or a guiding principle, the Holy Spirit urges everyone to join the love group. Leave the fear society, the us-versus-them club, the I'm-better-than-you bunch.

Why? Because God reminds us in Scripture that we are God's creation—we are one in Jesus Christ (Galatians 3:28). Christ's blood looks like your blood and my blood. His blood flowed for us all.

In spite of Grandpa, I love how unique and varied we all are. Being disabled and short in stature makes it tough for me to look down on anyone. I'd need to climb a tree like short Zacchaeus. If I did, Jesus would call me down and invite me to dinner. Thanks to Jesus, I'm changed by love.

"He said 'Love . . . as I have loved you.'
We cannot love too much."
—Amy Carmichael

When You Take Care of You

Therefore, my heart is glad and my tongue rejoices; my body also will rest secure,
—Psalm 16:9

That day, Mom called again for what seemed like the umpteenth time. "Can you come over right now? I'm out of diet soda."

Inwardly, I fumed. Mom's demands piled on top of my hectic schedule.

Grandchildren needed rides to sports practice. Thrice weekly hemodialysis weakened my husband, so I managed the finances, took the car for oil changes, and set out the trash. Even the cat and the bunny clamored for attention. Had I remembered their breakfast that morning?

I had to admit I was too busy.

Most of my problems stemmed from my inability to say no. In our culture, women are expected to multitask. We work real jobs while we raise children and manage households. The rat race is alive and well as both women and men compete to climb social ladders or get ahead.

The harder I tried to keep my life going smoothly, the bumpier it seemed to become. Headaches plagued me. I'd forgotten one appointment and shown up to another on the wrong day. I prayed, asking God to help me, and one word floated across my mind. Rest.

Rest? How could I stop caring for my husband and my mother? The animals weren't going to feed themselves, and the grandkids grew up too fast to take a break. For every excuse I dreamed up, I kept coming back to rest.

I'm a doer and have never napped. I like staying busy. Still, I could almost hear God chuckling. *You do know that even I took a day off on the Sabbath, right?*

The light bulb switched on. God's rest might look different from the usual concept. Instead of forcing myself to lie down and do nothing, I could take time to meditate on Scripture. I could take a walk and marvel at my Father's world. I could sit and pray or daydream. Even better, in prayer, I could practice loving people who needed a lot more of it. Anything that helped recharge my batteries seemed to work.

All of the above increased my appreciation for God's loving care and spectacular creation. I still need to work on saying no to too many requests and activities. When obligations overwhelm, Jesus smiles and shakes his head, ready to let us climb upon his shoulders for a while. God's rest can be like a cool, watered garden, a place to inhale grace for busyness, and a soft, mossy bank to feel God's love filling our souls.

When Mom called again, she sounded frantic. "When are you coming over?"

I brought enough soda for two, and I relaxed as we watched the sunset burst into reds, oranges, and pinks.

"God's rest says: You are loved before you've done anything at all. You can stop. You are allowed to stop."
—Kate Bowler

When Relationships Heal

Do not judge, and you will not be judged. Do not condemn, and you will not be condemned. Forgive, and you will be forgiven.
—Luke 6:37

We had a falling out.

My half-sister had asked me to help her with a project she wanted to do, but I said I couldn't. At the time, I was caregiving for both my husband and my mother in addition to navigating health problems of my own.

I thought she'd say, "Let me know when it's a better time." Instead, she hurled a few choice words and then refused to communicate further.

At first, I thought we'd simply misunderstood one another. After all, we hadn't grown up together—I'd only found my biological father and family a few years earlier. Sis and I didn't know each other as well as if we'd been girls together in the same household.

I waited, hoping she'd get over her pique. But a year later, her last words to me were still the spicy curses she'd blasted. I could get over a spontaneous outburst. I say things I don't mean, too. The ghosting really hurt.

My sister lived in another city. I needed her to know I loved and forgave her, but she ignored my texts and calls. The raw spot in my heart insisted I keep trying to heal my relationship. But I didn't know how.

I prayed about it, and my sister's behavior began to make sense. Although I'd focused on my hurt at her attack, I saw that she was hurting too. What if she'd experienced my turning down her project as a rejection? What if, instead of *now is not a good time*, she'd heard *I'm not interested in getting to know you*?

We've heard that walking a mile in someone else's moccasins can help us understand others, especially if they're different or hostile. We feel justified withholding love from those who wronged us.

Jesus, in asking us to forgive, wants us to go further. Instead of saying we forgive yet we still harbor hurt or indignation, we can grow our capacity to love. To love even if they don't deserve it. To set aside tit for tat requires big love—God's love. Maybe this is part of what Paul means when he says his weakness is his strength. The world sees love as weakness, but the Lord knows love is powerful indeed.

I tried one last time to reach my sibling. When she answered the phone, my heart raced. What if she said meaner things or hung up on me? Words tumbled out as I explained about the timing of her request and my loaded plate at the time. "I'm still too busy," I said, "but let's work out something together. Okay?"

My sister remained quiet.

"I love you," I added.

Finally, she responded. "I love you too."

I broke into a grin. I think Jesus was smiling too.

"We can improve our relationships with others by leaps and bounds if we become encouragers instead of critics."
—Joyce Meyer

When Generational Trauma Heals

You shall not bow down to them or worship them; for I, the Lord your God, am a jealous God, punishing the children for the sin of the parents to the third and fourth generation of those who hate me,
—Exodus 20:5

In the eighteen-fifties, one of my relatives spent time in prison for horse stealing.

My family tree is riddled with addiction and mental illness, and I've worried that we have some sort of generational curse. Silly in modern times, right?

Not silly for me. Substance use and mental issues affect my children. It's been hard not to wonder, like ancient folks, if past wrongdoing made God want to punish us. Like the Scripture from the book of Exodus that mentions sins of a father extending to future generations, I've been in spiritual circles that explain any problems in terms of guilt and shame.

The idea of a generational curse led me to think God didn't like me much. Jesus was all right, but I felt frightened of the Father. I thought I'd never be able to outrun the "curse" of misguided interpretations.

Nothing like feeling doomed to bring you into a closer walk with the Lord.

For years, I was stuck in the Old Testament, where God appeared to be mean and angry with people. God seemed to be an erratic parent, and I was the child who never knew what kind of mood he'd be in when I came home.

Generational curses dovetailed nicely with the tendency to blame parents for wayward offspring. If drugs, alcohol, or sex sank their fangs into an innocent child, their parent obviously failed to train him up in the way he should go. When three out of four of my kids had trouble with addiction, I blamed myself as codependent and enabling.

Somehow, God finally got through to me.

I believed in Jesus, but I hadn't *belonged* to him. Until love proved too powerful against my worry, my defenses, my self-blame. I began to love my kids unconditionally. I loved them the way Jesus loved me. And the difference has been life-changing.

When loved ones suffer from diseases, addiction, or other shortcomings, we can quickly jump back to that OT wrath-filled God. Yet if we plant ourselves firmly at Jesus' feet, we find him commanding us to love others as we love ourselves. We can still have boundaries that keep us safe and our values intact without sacrificing our love. Loving instead of shaming takes some practice, but Jesus wants to help us carry that change (Matthew 11:28). Because Christ doesn't love us once we change. He loves us, so we *can* change.

As I practice this kind of love, the guilty shame of a generational curse evaporates. I can stand before both the Old and New Testament God. The Holy Spirit opens my heart, and I gratefully receive blessings instead of cursing, knowing that God is love.

"Words of kindness are more healing to a drooping heart than balm or honey."
—Sarah Fielding

When Whataboutism Arises

The other woman said, "No! The living one is
my son; the dead one is yours." But the first one
insisted, "No! The dead one is yours; the living one
is mine." And so they argued before the king.
—I Kings 3:22

At the store, my payment had been declined.

My husband had spent too much at the bar. I stayed up late to confront him.

When he came home, I said he'd been drinking.

He yelled, "What about your spending spree?"

"What about your breath?" I could smell alcohol.

He came closer. "What about your new dress?"

"What about Scotch? That's more expensive than any outfit." And so it went. I became so mad that I eventually threw a jar of yellow mustard at him. Luckily, it missed his head but stained the wall.

We tried to hurt each other with whataboutism.

The scene reminded me of a time when I'd tried to talk my way out of punishment. I was around six or seven, and on a hot Arizona day, I turned on the garden hose to get a drink. I ran off to play without turning off the faucet and flooded the front yard.

When my mother asked me about it, I admitted I'd forgotten to turn off the hose. Then I blurted, "But what about Sissy? *She* walked across the rug with muddy shoes."

When a discussion starts to go sideways, we can feel the heat and try to save face. If we're mistaken about facts, distraction helps to convince us that we're not wrong. I used whataboutism to wriggle out of accountability in hopes of minimizing or escaping consequences.

Of course, our loving God knows the real story. Yet we often feel the need to prove we're right or that the other side is wrong.

What if there's another way to disagree without alienating others or evading responsibility? We can allow people to be wrong.

I could have held my temper and waited until morning to discuss our finances and my husband's drinking habits. Instead of needing to prove my point, I could have let go of trying to force him to admit wrongdoing in the middle of the night.

God asks us not to let the sun go down on our anger (Ephesians 4:26). To start an argument solely for the purpose of proving someone else is wrong cancels opportunities to love our neighbors as God loves them.

In the morning, my husband and I kissed and made up. We promised to be more transparent with each other. For years, the yellow mustard stain on our wall reminded me to let people be wrong. And confess my own wrongdoings to God who is ever merciful and forgiving of sins.

"Whataboutism is a straw man argument."
—Shayne Silvers

When Tit for Tat Doesn't Work

Likewise, the tongue is a small part of the body,
but it makes great boasts. Consider what a
great forest is set on fire by a small spark.
—James 3:5

You did it!"

"It's all your fault!"

When they disagreed, my sons yelled insults at each other.

They tried to push one another toward more anger. Once, I had to get between them to keep fists from flying.

Later, when I asked one why he couldn't settle differences without fighting, he said, "Mom. You don't poke the bear."

I shook my head. "No, son. There's always an adult way to talk things out without coming to blows."

I thought about how our culture teaches boys and men to be strong and hyper-masculine. Movies, video games, and television seem to glorify violence. My husband and I never encouraged these influences, but he was a combat veteran Marine who loved war movies. Besides, we couldn't keep our sons from all modern media.

They were adults now, but they seemed to be sucked into those manosphere ideas. I cannot tolerate violence of any kind. Since they live in my home, I didn't have the heart to put them out on the street, but I needed a peaceful home. What was the answer?

I ran to God to recenter my discomfort. In Matthew 5:38, Jesus says, "You have heard that it was said, 'Eye for eye, and tooth for tooth.' But I tell you, do not resist an evil person. If anyone slaps you on the right cheek, turn to them the other cheek also." The Lord's wisdom strikes down the human tendency toward war and violence as a way to settle scores.

Yet violence often seems to be winning. Turning the other cheek can be incredibly difficult, especially when tempers flare. I'm not innocent either—I've screamed at my kids for screaming at each other.

Perhaps the difficulty comes from the beginning of anger. In James 4:6, we read

"The tongue also is a fire, a world of evil among the parts of the body. It corrupts the whole body, sets the whole course of one's life on fire, and is itself set on fire by hell." Every person has the potential to say unkind or untrue things.

When our speech lights the fire of anger, we have more guidance. Ephesians 4:26 says, "In your anger do not sin": Do not let the sun go down while you are still angry."

Refreshing myself on what God says about anger helps me think twice before I react or reply. There can be righteous anger, but I don't want to use anger or labeling to hurt another person. As a disabled person, I know how painful generalizing can be.

With my adult sons, change must come from them, so I set a boundary. If they conduct themselves as adults without escalating threats or slurs, they can stay. If not, my sons will have to find another place to be.

Since setting that boundary, no more vicious verbal or physical fights have happened. Daily, I tell them how loved they are, by me, the family, and the Lord. They know that I'm the bear they shouldn't poke.

An eye for an eye leaves everybody blind.
—Martin Luther King Jr.

When You Can't Catch a Break

My comfort in my suffering is this: Your promise preserves my life.
—Psalm 119:50

I laid my head on the steering wheel and turned the key again. *Please, Lord*, I prayed.

But all I heard was a series of clicks. "Gimme a break!" Anger rose up my spine, and my prayer changed to *Why me, Lord? Stupid battery.*

That day, nothing had gone right. I overslept. Still groggy, I made my coffee too sweet. Then the car wouldn't start. I'd be late for my appointment. And my attitude sank into resentment.

One of my loved ones struggles with depression. He often says that every good deed he does for friends comes back to bite him. Sadly, he often feels doomed, like life itself has it out for him. He often reminds me of Winnie the Pooh's donkey friend, Eeyore.

I have had seasons where it seemed as if I couldn't catch a break. Times when I was sure everyone else's life was smooth while mine was a roller coaster of unfortunate events. No matter how I tried, my days went sideways.

Whether we're depressed or just having a no-good day, we sometimes feel like life is plotting against us. Blaming inanimate objects like dead batteries is a sure step toward resentment and bitterness.

My mother used to remind me that life isn't fair. But I still thought I shouldn't have to suffer. The more things went wrong, the harder I tried to control them. If I went too far, I ended up feeling entitled and mad at the world.

When tough things happen, I always have a choice. I can be upset and feel slighted, or I can choose to accept that life is hard and give it my best and most prayerful shot. By taking away the focus on what I deserve or what I think is owed to me, I can concentrate on getting through hardships, calamities, or a dead battery. And when I stumble under the weight of trouble, Jesus promises that I won't ever be hefting bad things alone (John:14:18). For me, somehow knowing that I am deeply loved gives me courage. God gives me strength I didn't know I needed and carries me through awful stuff.

Saint Paul says in Romans that our sufferings lead to perseverance, character, and hope Romans 5:3. Walking through the fire with Jesus helps us grow the hope that no matter what happens, God will never abandon us (Hebrews 13:5b).

I got the car battery fixed and rescheduled my missed appointment. Although inconvenient, the morning wasn't a total loss. I leaned on God to get through, and God showered me with love to spare.

When that depressed loved one asked why I didn't make it to the appointment, I smiled and said, "Oh, gimme a break." We laughed.

"If you're going through hell, keep going."
—Winston Churchill

When You Don't Feel Accepted

If we live, we live for the Lord; and if we die, we die for the Lord. So, whether we live or die, we belong to the Lord.
—Romans 14:8

I stood on the outside edge of a clutch of seventh-grade girls. They were the popular kids—Pat and Yolanda ruled the playground. A few others—Connie, Bonnie, and Peggy—belonged to the clique. These girls were top athletes, wore the latest styles, and claimed popular boys as crushes.

And then there was me.

I did a pretty good job of hiding my paralysis and tried to keep up with hairstyles and clothes. But I loved school and that set me apart from kids who looked down on brainiacs. Though I could be funny, my parents had strict rules that restricted attending parties or hanging out unsupervised. I seemed to have one foot in the group and one outside.

I held out hope that I'd be accepted until one day in physical education class. We ran laps around the track while the teacher timed us. Desperate for the approval of the athletic girls, I ran as fast as I could. By the second lap, my polio-weakened lungs burned, but I was determined to impress.

Anyone who's ever felt as if they weren't accepted understands the lonely, hollow feeling. The longing to be seen, valued, and to belong is a fundamental trait of being human.

God knows we all need nurturing companionship and created us to need one another. If not, perhaps Jesus might not have placed so much importance on loving one's neighbor. Love helps us accept one another without judgment or scorn, without us versus them, without being in or out of a chosen group. As many have observed, we all bleed the same red blood. We're far more alike than different. God's love empowers us to see past differences and accept whomever our neighbor might be.

Some folks are difficult, no doubt about it. Some people we must love from afar. But every time we extend grace to another, we're helping that person see that they, too, belong to God's family. And we feel God's arms around us, saying, "I accept you too."

Running on that track, with another lap to go, I'd hoped the "in crowd" was watching. Until I started seeing spots and everything went black.

I regained consciousness as one of the most popular girls tried to help me up. Gripped by shame, I feared I'd never belong. The cool kids would never accept me.

Then Pat, the leader of the group, came and whispered. "C'mon, you can do it."

I brushed off my scraped knees, grinned, and jogged over the finish line.

"True belonging doesn't require you to change who you are; it requires you to be who you are."
—Brene Brown

When You Don't Feel Appreciated

> But Martha was distracted by all the preparations that had to be made. She came to him and asked, "Lord, don't you care that my sister has left me to do the work by myself? Tell her to help me!"
> —Luke 10:40

My husband of forty-seven years may have thought of himself as head of household, but sometimes he infuriated me.

One year, while doing our taxes, filing jointly, he turned to me and said, "I put down your occupation as housewife."

He didn't understand why I became so upset.

Although I did the things housewives do, I thought of myself as a professional with college degrees, having taught in public and private schools. I'd retired and embarked upon a quest to be a published author. The last thing I wanted to be known for was mopping floors or cleaning toilets.

Apparently, to dear hubby, my career as a freelance writer didn't qualify as a legitimate occupation.

My husband was the love of my life, and our marriage skewed toward the traditional. We raised our four kids in much the same way that my folks raised me. My husband mowed the lawn and emptied the trash. I cooked, cleaned, and did a jillion other household tasks.

Like most women in our society, I identified with Martha's complaint about her sister Mary. And like Martha, I felt unappreciated. I wondered if Jesus' answer—that Mary had chosen the better part—secretly made Martha fume.

Martha thought Jesus was saying that Martha's tasks weren't important. Cooking and cleaning and making sure Jesus' cup was full weren't as good as Mary's actions. I understand the anger of a woman who felt unappreciated.

When nobody noticed how hard she was working, Martha became angry. When would it be her turn to relax at Jesus' feet? She thought no one cared.

Now and then, everyone feels unappreciated. We work our tail off, yet others ignore our efforts. Even worse, supercritical people nitpick our hard work. Then, like Martha, we have a choice. We can either keep working to our own standards or become bitter and resentful.

God offers a third way. Jesus didn't tell Mary to help. He didn't say Martha couldn't *also* sit at His feet. Jesus didn't cluck and say *work harder* or *you missed a spot*. The real choice wasn't about her envy of Mary. Maybe it was Martha's own pride saying nobody could do the stuff as well as she could.

I didn't like being called a housewife. I was better than that. But this story shows me that *all* jobs are important. At any time, I can put down the dusting rag and sit at Jesus' feet. I appreciate that.

"When we are angry or depressed in our creativity, we have misplaced our power. We have allowed someone else to determine our worth, and then we are angry at being undervalued."

—Julia Margaret Cameron

When Disaster Strikes

I knew that you are a gracious and compassionate
God, slow to anger and abounding in love, a
God who relents from sending calamity.
—Jonah 4:2b

The worst disaster in my life came the day I went to a rehab center to visit my husband.

We'd already been through ten years of crises. First heart problems, then an unfortunate cholesterol embolism. The result was complete kidney failure, requiring weekly hemodialysis for the rest of his life.

As a former Marine, my husband was brave and didn't complain about the three-hour, three-times weekly sessions to clean his blood. But kidney failure is a complicated and cruel disease. He became the poster patient at our local kidney center. And despite his frequent hospitalizations, surgeries, and painful procedures, we worked as a team to keep him going.

But his heart wasn't finished wreaking havoc. He survived a major stroke and battled chronic heart failure. When he'd been on dialysis for ten years, a serious car crash nearly killed him.

After battling back from the accident, my sweetie resumed his routine. Shortly thereafter, he was hospitalized again. Doctors said most dialysis patients live no longer than about ten years. Yet he defied the odds and transferred to a rehabilitation facility.

That afternoon, I drove to the rehab to sign papers. I walked into his room and froze. My beautiful, blue-eyed Marine stared straight ahead, unresponsive. The image is burned into my memory.

Whether flood, fire, storm, or death, we have our own calamities and disasters to remember. Everyone grieves loss differently, but disasters leave us feeling empty, heartbroken, and traumatized, sometimes for life.

Even those who say they don't believe often call on God to help in the throes of the worst thing imaginable. We cry out for rescue, for comfort, for some way to make sense out of life's awful days.

Independence evaporates as we realize that we can't handle this crisis alone. Humbled in the face of need, we're forced to let God carry us through this tragedy, too. God shows up to help through our friends, families, and perfect strangers. We reject the helpers God sends us at our peril. Big trouble teaches us to open our hearts to big help, big comfort, and big love.

In that moment at the rehab, I knew immediately—my husband was having another stroke. He would never recover, and I was devastated.

Yet now I have the experience of helping, loving, and comforting others. I treasure the memory of those gorgeous blue eyes. They will always remind me of the love we shared. The big love I can pass on to everyone who faces disaster assures me that God will indeed carry us through.

"A real friend walks in when the rest of the world walks out."

—Walter Winchell

When You're a Caregiver

For he has not despised or scorned the suffering
of the afflicted one; he has not hidden his face
from him but has listened to his cry for help.
—Psalm 22:24

My TV won't turn on." Mom's voice over the phone sounded shrill. "Come over and fix it for me."

I glanced at the clock. It was 10:00 p.m.

My mother had moved to my city to be near me. She was eighty-nine, starting to show signs of dementia, and her demands took a toll on me.

Caring for a parent must be one of the hardest jobs we do. I cared for my mother as she aged, as well as my husband as he coped with kidney disease. Add in my grown children's issues, and many days, I felt like the world's caregiver.

Mom was difficult. She often was demanding and a tad selfish. She called me multiple times each day from her independent living facility, complaining about what she needed right away or insisting I rush over immediately.

My husband's three-time-weekly dialysis treatments, frequent hospitalizations, and general day-to-day needs pressed in. He wasn't demanding like my mother, but I wanted to help him as much as possible.

I felt stretched so thin I thought I'd snap in two. Keeping everyone happy was an exhausting and full-time job. My own health worsened, and I became resentful. I prayed about my attitude and my workload, but I was headed for disaster.

Every day, I told myself I could do anything for a few hours. But many times, caregiving was twenty-four-seven. I wanted to be a good caregiver, but I was burnt out.

As our parents age, more of us will become caregivers. Those with special needs children or family members, those who do caregiving for a job, know the rigors and challenges of caregiving. Our God is willing and able to give our souls a break whenever we're growing closer to that burnout.

I first had to learn that while my intentions were good, I was no Mother Teresa. I didn't have to do anything more than my best. As I learned to stop rushing toward perfect caregiving, Jesus swooped me up and carried me through the parts I thought I'd never survive.

God helped me understand that Mom's demands arose from fear. I concentrated on soothing her fear with songs, laughter, and Scriptures. I poured extra love into every task. And when I felt overwhelmed, I discovered that by leaning on Jesus, I could be better organized and set boundaries to preserve my health and sanity.

That night at 10:00 p.m., I told Mom I'd be over in the morning to fix the TV.

"Let's sing some songs to help you sleep," I said.

The fear in her voice dissolved as we sang of God's love.

"Caregiving often calls us to lean into love we didn't know was possible."

—Tia Walker

When You Need Confidence

"But blessed is the one who trusts in the
Lord, whose confidence is in him.
—Jeremiah 17:7

My knees shook as I mounted the school stage.

At age fourteen, I was about to sing a folk song at a summer music camp talent show in Northern Arizona. I knew the adage about imagining the audience in their underwear. But I was scared stiff.

I tried to slow my breathing and shot up an emergency prayer. *Please, dear God, don't let me flub this song.* The accompaniment began. My mouth felt too dry.

I wanted to be a professional singer. People said I had a good singing voice. My grandmother, a music teacher, had helped send me to this elite music camp at a university. Being around so many talented high schoolers encouraged my dreams. But I quickly learned that confidence was my biggest lack.

Whether it's fear of public speaking, performing, or making social media videos, most of us shake in our boots if we must get in front of an audience. Clubs and courses abound to practice public speaking and build confidence.

Starting a new career or job can trigger feelings of uncertainty. New parents often face a lack of confidence in their abilities to raise a child. While some people thrive in the limelight, most of us have areas of our lives where confidence flags.

Confident people often rise to the top of competitions. Others fake it till they make it. But God offers a different kind of confidence that is rooted in Christ's love.

I've misunderstood this confidence to mean *bully my way* to the top. If I think I'm better than others, a false type of confidence emerges. But by staying grounded in God's love, by attempting to live every moment by following Jesus' example to love God and neighbor, I come closer to the divine confidence found in God.

Building this kind of confidence comes from resting in the knowledge that God loves us unconditionally, whether we succeed or fail. We can be certain that Jesus will carry us through anything and never abandon or forsake us.

This confidence enables us to help others in need, without worrying that there isn't enough. To be more like Jesus and freely give of our time, possessions, and love to the marginalized. We can set aside competition where there are winners and losers and consider every person as made in God's image.

As I opened my mouth to sing that folk song, I felt God's presence beside me, nodding. I could dare to give my best performance, whether the audience sat in their undies or not. As I exited the stage, I thought I heard God clapping his appreciation.

"You are enough, just as you are."
—Meghan Markle

When You Fail, Big Time

Have mercy on me, O God, according to your unfailing love;
according to your great compassion blot out my transgressions.
—Psalm 51:1

When she finally got through to me, my only daughter was in tears. I'd just returned from a conference where there was no cell service, and she was frantic. After less than four years, her marriage was broken and unfixable.

My heart broke into a million pieces. Although I'd had doubts, I wanted her to succeed. The shame in her voice was unmistakable. She'd failed big time. Her marriage was falling apart.

Years ago, I'd failed that same way. While my husband was on a trip to Costa Rica with his boss, I fled from San Diego to Denver with two small children in tow. The first thing I did at my folks' home was sit on the floor and sob.

"I can't believe I failed." Tears ran down my cheeks. I rocked back and forth, feeling like I was to blame for making poor choices.

My daughter and I felt an immense load of guilt. Yes, our respective mates drank to excess and could be verbally abusive.

But the feelings of failure persisted.

Our society urges us to be successful. We're taught that success means never-ending progress toward more, never less. Self-help books promise to help us be more prosperous, have more possessions and prestige. To never lose.

There's nothing wrong with success. Most of us work hard to live a success-filled life. Yet we're also expected to make correct choices every time. Whether a marriage, a job, or a friendship, things that go sideways convince us that we're failures.

If we don't overcome our guilt and shame, trying again may be too difficult. We lose hope. Our lives shrivel until we call ourselves losers.

But failing big-time never results in losing the love of God. In fact, when we look around and there aren't many shoulders to cry on, Jesus stands ready to cushion the blows we're dealt. Whether we run to him through Scripture or prayer or just your own sobs, God invites us to lean on those Everlasting Arms.

Jesus comforts us, whispering that because we are made in God's image, we aren't really failures at all. To help develop persistence, hope, and character, cling to God who loves us and carries us through.

My daughter is happily remarried, and I reunited with my husband. Our failures helped us gain wisdom in making better choices. We learned how to reject false guilt and shame and move instead toward forgiveness.

The day my daughter called with her news, I comforted her, saying she wasn't alone. God would never leave her nor forsake her. "God carried me through, and God will carry you too." I'm thankful that our big God helps us survive big fails.

"The secret of life is to fall seven times and to get up eight times."

—Paulo Coelho

When Love Feels Far Away

Turn to me and be gracious to me, for
I am lonely and afflicted.
—Psalm 25:16

My first steady boyfriend came during high school, where we both sang in a band. He was a real talent, and I was mesmerized by his impressive baritone, great guitar skills, and dreamy blue eyes. He told me that the first day we met to rehearse, he told his buddies he called dibs on the chick with the red knee socks.

As teen romances go, much of what I called love was really doing whatever I needed to break away from my parents. I liked my crush, but because of my paralyzed arm, I secretly didn't think I was worthy of true love. When you're eighteen and disabled, you hold all sorts of fantasies about relationships.

And it didn't help that a different guy said he'd totally date me—*if* it wasn't for that bum arm.

Insecure and longing to find that one soulmate, I convinced myself that the only place I'd ever find true love was at . . . a laundromat.

I taught myself to sing in front of a big audience. But I hugged the wall at parties, and my throat closed up when meeting a new acquaintance. A failure at mingling, maybe I'd be lovable if someone else was so broken that they hung out at the coin-op too.

Now, at the other end of life, I'm widowed. I never found that one true love while washing clothes. Love did eventually find me, but not in the way I imagined.

During my forty-seven-year marriage, I rarely felt head-over-heels in love with my husband. In fact, we fought as much as we made up. We made it work, though, through teamwork, therapy work, and plain hard work.

Occasionally, I still fantasize about soulmates. What might it be like to love and be loved so completely? Does my disability really prevent me from realizing such a profound and deep union? Does my special someone even exist?

We long for true love. God is love, and we're made in God's image. We're wired to both give and receive love. Whether it's a failing marriage, a broken friendship, or an estranged family member, when love is far away, we feel loss. A gaping maw of emptiness threatens to swallow us whole. Sometimes we retreat into impossible fantasies or blame our flaws for our loneliness.

Yet love has been there all along. God's love is so deep, so real that our insecurities and self-doubts can't snuff out the bright light. God doesn't demand that we meet in a laundromat.

Come as you are, the God of love says. However you are, wherever you are, come. As the Scriptures say, taste and see that the Lord is good (Psalm 34:8). The closer you draw to God, the closer love draws to you. Our gracious God longs to be your soulmate forever.

"To love and be loved is to feel the sun from both sides."
—David Viscott

When You Try to Change

The Lord is not slow in keeping his promise, as some understand slowness. Instead, he is patient with you, not wanting anyone to perish, but everyone to come to repentance.
—II Peter 3:9

As a young woman, I was always dieting. I wasn't obese, but a stubborn ten to fifteen pounds settled around my hips and refused to be evicted. I tried every diet out there. Once, I tried to make popcorn on my stovetop using mineral oil. I was ridiculous, but I just couldn't stop dieting.

The more I tried to change my body to please others, the more I binged on ice cream from the carton. My figure was decent, but I wasn't Barbie. I wanted to change for all the wrong reasons.

Change is hard. And change is life. In the second half of life, I'm more aware than ever of change and its consequences. In ways, if we don't change, we're doomed. If we do change, it's even worse.

Women know about that Proverbs Thirty-one Excellent Gal, and we attempt to do it all. Men are pressured to fit a macho ideal. Even the apostle Paul griped about not being able to change. In 2 Corinthians 12:7b, Paul says, "Therefore, in order to keep me from becoming conceited, I was given a thorn in my flesh."

Did that mean God laughed at pathetic human weaklings, the ones who tried but failed to stop smoking, stop swearing, or stop any other vice? I've imagined all of heaven shaking their heads and pointing to the losers who couldn't change habits.

No. God is more interested in seeing us change things, such as our penchant for fear into kindness and compassion. God cheers when we transform from crabby and cramped to open and loving.

Real change happens when our minds, hearts, and souls enlarge God's kingdom right here on earth. When we change swords into ploughs and lions lie down with lambs.

I once thought I couldn't be in Jesus' club because I wasn't good enough. I didn't study the Bible enough or pray enough or repeat the right slogans. But I've found, after many years of failing, that Jesus didn't only love people once they'd changed (fill in your choice of bad habits). He loves all of us so that we *can* change.

Change can be hard. Sometimes we stumble and give up. God says when we're weak, then we're strong (2 Corinthians 12:10). In surrender, we're free to love, to care, to turn our gaze away from ourselves and toward neighbors who need loving.

Even at my age, I still worry about overeating. But when I start to berate my bad food choices or fret that I won't be wearing a bathing suit, I remember that Jesus is carrying me all the way from Dietsville to You're Beautiful Town.

"I alone cannot change the world, but I can cast a stone across the waters to create many ripples."

—Mother Teresa

When You Stop Judging

"Do not judge, or you too will be judged.
—Matthew 7:1

Old enough to be my mother, my friend was a brilliant writer. But she could be bombastic. One day, as we were shopping, I commented that a plus-sized woman ahead of us in line shouldn't wear tight leggings with giant flowers printed on them.

My friend wore a shocked expression. "Aren't you just the ugly little judge!"

It was my turn to look shocked. Me? A judge? And not a particularly pretty one? I'm sure I turned red.

As a disabled person, I should have known better. As a woman, a human, a Jesus follower, I'd judged that lady in a petty, critical way.

I was quiet after that, but inside I fumed. Didn't life force us to make judgments all day, every day? To go this way or that way? To do this or that? To judge something safe or dangerous?

Most of us have judged badly at one time or another. We often make excuses when things go wrong or when we have regrets. *I wasn't ready for that putt. I was only trying to help. That guy deserved what he got.* Even when the pronouncement never reaches its intended target, like giving unsolicited fashion advice to a total stranger.

We must have laws and rules to keep us safe and to guide expectations. If we put money into a soda machine, we want to be sure we'll get some soda. And when life gets dangerous, we want those rules enforced.

Yet most of us aren't real judges, the kind with robes and gavels. We can avoid our judgy moments. Refer to Jesus' two simple laws: Love the lord your God and love your neighbor as yourself. If you're like me, you need constant reminders of these two rules. All the law and the prophets hang on these babies, people. Review as often as necessary. Like every second.

Some people add these questions: Is it kind? Is it helpful? Necessary? If you get a no on any of these, rethink your motives.

The world wasn't going to blow up because a woman wore unflattering pants. The only thing that exploded that day was my secret ambition to make myself look better by tearing down someone else. I definitely don't want those in the queue behind me to think catty thoughts about my body. I do want to become more like Jesus every day.

I could have told my friend she was judging me for judging that stranger. Did she really need to add *little* and *ugly*? Ouch. But her words still echo in my mind whenever I rev up my judgy self. They remind me to concentrate on the *love thy neighbor* part and avoid being the ugly little judge.

"The least amount of judging we can do,
the better off we are."
—Michael J. Fox

When It's Okay to be Ordinary

For we are God's handiwork, created in Christ Jesus to do good works, which God prepared in advance for us to do.
—Ephesians 2:10

Karen was an ordinary kid with mousy brown hair, goofy eyeglasses, and a mouthful of braces. Shy and quiet, Karen was the butt of the popular kids' jokes. Our seventh-grade teacher always asked her to speak up when called upon.

I desperately wanted to be a part of the popular crowd. I never made fun of Karen myself, but I laughed at the jabs the cool kids made. Nobody in grade seven would admit to befriending such a nobody.

Then Peggy, one of the girls in the cool crowd, invited me to her birthday sleepover. I felt so important. Before the party, I spent hours deciding what I'd wear and figuring out the perfect gift to bring. I rehearsed what I'd talk about—something sure to get attention; juicy gossip that could earn me a spot in the inner circle.

The evening of the party, I practically turned myself inside out with jitters. Did I look stylish enough? Were my pjs cute? What if someone pointed out my paralyzed left arm? But I went anyway.

Peggy, an athletic girl with naturally curly hair, seemed glad to see me. Sleeping bag in hand, I trundled in with all the rest of the girls, then stopped short. On the floor amidst piles of pillows and blankets, Karen sat alone.

I hadn't heard about The Plan. They'd agreed ahead of time to completely ignore Karen. No one spoke to her or even made eye contact. They jabbered among themselves. Karen looked miserable.

In our culture of good, better, and best, we often think we can't be ordinary. Everyone's sure they must be exceptional in every way. An average grade feels shameful. We must use the best doctors, hairstylists, mechanics, and attend prestigious schools. Or else . . . what exactly?

We want to be unique, not ordinary.

This kind of pursuit of excellence is exhausting and can lead to exaggeration or even outright fabrication. But God has knit each of us uniquely to contribute to the entire body. As Paul points out, if everyone is an eye, nobody's left to hear (I Corinthians 12:17). We don't always feel it, but in Christ, nobody's too cool, and nobody's too ordinary for God's love.

That night at the sleepover, all the girls finally bedded down, and the room got quiet. But I heard Karen, softly whimpering. Jesus calmly carried my heart to a place where I ached for this ordinary girl. Before I'd set my sights on the cool kids, all I'd ever wanted was to be not disabled—ordinary. I reached out a hand and gently squeezed hers.

I realized I no longer wanted to be in the popular clique of girls who were mean on purpose. I'd rather be Karen's uniquely ordinary friend.

"The secret to life is finding joy in ordinary things. I'm interested in happiness."
— Ruth Reichl

When You See Jesus in Everyone

For as in Adam all die, so in Christ all will be made alive.
—I Corinthians 15:22

I fast-walked down a busy city street. I'd heard this place was crime-ridden—I could get mugged, robbed, or worse. A man walking the other way bumped my shoulder. My heart clutched, and I shot up an emergency prayer. *Lord, please don't let this guy hurt me.*

I prayed for safety, but if I were honest, Jesus was only an idea. I believed, considered myself born again, studied my Bible and attended church regularly. Yet, I believed God was out there somewhere, always watching to see if I goofed up. I was supposed to be walking with, talking with, and praying with Jesus. But I didn't feel very close to God or the Only Son.

I kept these feelings private. I went through the motions and tried harder to be in love with Jesus. Nothing worked.

Some Christians warn against emotions altogether. Danger lurks when people prey upon others in the name of religion. Yet I know Christians whose professed love of the Lord appears so genuine, so complete, so experiential. The command to *love the Lord your God with all your heart, mind, and soul* tugged at me. I wanted that total love experience too.

We're nudged toward a bigger commitment to Christ, a fuller, more complete life in him. We seek this closer union in different ways—through Bible Study, traditions, and prayer. We want a personal savior, but many of us don't know how to cultivate an authentic personal relationship with Jesus.

Some may be content with their current relationship with God, but I wanted more than belief. I wanted to be Jesus' bestie or at least be able to say he's a true friend.

When we accept a belief in the Triune God, we're taught to believe that Jesus was both divine and human. But belief is mostly the stuff of our thoughts. How can we also transform our hearts so that we believe *and* belong?

For me, a good place to start was with the second command to *love your neighbor as yourself.* I couldn't help noticing how Jesus edged closer whenever I helped someone in need. Suddenly, the words, "*for it is in giving that we receive*" and "*I can do all things through Christ who strengthens me* make much more sense. God's love floods our being when we recognize Jesus in everything and everyone.

When that stranger bumped into me, I froze for a moment, wondering if I should run. But my gaze met his eyes, a beautiful brown tinged with great sadness. Suddenly, there was Jesus, looking out of a random guy's face. I see the Lord everywhere now, in the most unlikely people I meet. And I know I belong to him.

"We belong to each other. We are sister and brother. Born to love one another."
—Garth Brooks

When You Practice Peace

Peace I leave with you; my peace I give you. I do not give to you as the world gives. Do not let your hearts be troubled and do not be afraid.
—John 14:27

My son and I argued. Our home was anything but peaceful.

"I was too," he shouted and slammed his bedroom door.

I yelled after him. "No, you weren't!" I was ready to explode.

"Not true!"

"Yes, it is!" I was angry. He was wrong. I was so right. We both fumed in silence. No peace was in sight.

I sat at the kitchen table, stewing. As I sat there, I felt God's presence. A question floated across my mind. What had my response to my son's words accomplished?

When we disagree with another person, it's easy to feel we must prove we're right. Civil discourse, in today's social climate, seems rare. We surround ourselves with only those who agree with us and feel that any other opinion is wrong.

When we group ourselves only with people who think as we do, we may believe we experience peace. But is it really the sort of peace that Jesus encouraged us to practice?

The famous Scripture to "not let the sun go down on your anger" (Ephesians 4:26) is shoved aside when righteous indignation takes over. When we're so certain that we're right, we can't hold space for any other point of view. Listening goes out the window. We become more separated from each other than ever.

When Jesus gives his peace, it passes all understanding. I take this to partly mean that real peace leaps over right and wrong and runs to love. Love of God. Love of neighbor.

Jesus' peace is a place where love triumphs, a place where we listen to others and disagree without insulting one another. This peace requires us to become vulnerable to the slings and arrows of daring to love, knowing we may not be accepted.

Practicing peace doesn't mean being a sycophant or a doormat, either. Maybe that's why, when offering us his peace, he adds *don't be afraid.* Jesus had strong opinions, too. But because he came from a heart of love, he could remain vulnerable and authentic and disagree without being disagreeable.

Peace that passes understanding, peace that we can practice without fear, goes beyond right or wrong. With this kind of peace, we can allow others to be wrong. That's right. Peace to allow the person we disagree with to be as absolutely incorrect as you think they are.

That's what I heard God saying to me that day. "You don't have to prove you're right. You can let him be wrong."

Anger dissipating, I stood up from the table and went to my son's door. I knocked softly. "I'm sorry I was yelling," I said. "I wasn't listening very well."

Out of the corner of my eye, I thought I saw Jesus' smile.

"God cannot give us a happiness and peace apart from Himself, because it is not there. There is no such thing."

—C.S. Lewis

When You Serve Others

Each of you should use whatever gift you have
received to serve others, as faithful stewards
of God's grace in its various forms.
—I Peter 4:10

As a young mom to four children, including a set of twins, I longed for help. My husband was busy working, but I couldn't go back to teaching school yet—childcare costs would outweigh my income.

At that time, we'd just moved to the Pacific Northwest from Southern California, and so far, my support group was tiny. Women from my new church stepped up, but I felt awkward asking for help. When the church director asked me to volunteer for nursery duty, I thought I might faint.

Without a car, free time, or a good night's sleep, there was no way I could do one more thing. Our two boys were just entering school age, and the premature twins needed something approximately every minute.

A few years earlier, when I first became born again, the church I'd attended sang a song that included the words, "Let's forget about ourselves." The chorus was a reminder to think of others and serve them as we serve the Lord.

Now in our new residence, no one except my husband knew how exhausted I was. I begged God to show me how I could be a nursery attendant without dozing off or cracking.

These days, just about everybody I know is stretched impossibly thin. Women especially, still try to achieve Super Mom status. To make ends meet, most households must have two incomes. Household chores and child-rearing are stacked on top of full schedules.

And many must feel as I did. How do you serve God and still manage to do it all?

A friend confided that she was close to collapsing under the strain. Constant migraines, trouble sleeping, and irritability were a few of her symptoms. Between her career, family, and her longing to serve God, she was ready to fall apart.

I had to smile, remembering those long nights comforting two howling babies. Back then, I did a lot of praying at three a.m. As I recalled those tough days and nights, my friend was incredulous. She asked, "How'd you do it all?"

I laughed. "I didn't do it all. But God said okay." The answer to both our dilemmas was that when I couldn't go another step, Jesus carried me. I was raising kids to love God while praying for people's needs. And that was enough.

The day I had to say no to the deacon's request, I was afraid I'd be seen as selfish or worse. But the deacon said she understood.

"Thanks," I said, checking the time. The twins' next feeding was soon. To my surprise, the deacon asked if she could come and give me a few hours' break. I said yes before the babies awoke and the routine started all over again. I praised God for helping me forget about myself.

"When we give cheerfully and accept gratefully, everyone is blessed."

—Maya Angelou

When You See Beyond Rules

And the Lord said, "I will cause all my goodness to pass in front of you, and I will proclaim my name, the Lord, in your presence. I will have mercy on whom I will have mercy, and I will have compassion on whom I will have compassion.
—Exodus 33:19

I stood at the lunch buffet at a Christian conference, speaking privately to my companion as I piled fresh strawberries and cantaloupe chunks on my plate. "Yes," I said, "I think God can be both he and she."

My friend chuckled, and we found a spot to eat our meal before we each headed off to teach writing classes that afternoon.

Later, I was informed that I needed to review the organization's statement of faith. If I didn't, they wouldn't need me to teach after all.

I was confused. The organizers explained that my comment about God had raised eyebrows. I hadn't grown up in a conservative church and didn't realize that my comment was offensive. I believed that my God was big enough to embrace different views.

Perhaps. But the conferees weren't as tolerant. I went back to my room, weighing my options. I could apologize and joke that I didn't know my *hes* from my *shes*. Or I could defend my remark and walk out.

Some people seem to live by the book. Sometimes, we can be the ones who are uncomfortable when others do things differently. Our families, faith, and friends shape our world views.

Most of us dislike nitpicking, and sadly, many don't act when major rules are disregarded. We loathe the stereotypical mother-in-law saying, "You missed a spot," and resent those who glide through life without consequences. What does God expect of us?

I don't know every answer, but I do know that God isn't always waiting to catch us red-handed. We all need God's love more than ever when we encounter rulebreakers large and teeny-tiny. And we certainly must grow our capacity to act in love when world-class wrong happens before our eyes.

Discernment is the best way to react. We need three things to be good rule-parsers: to be open to at least hearing opposing views, to wisely weigh the rule's importance. And above all, we must have love in deciding what, if anything, to do about it.

I see a vast difference between accidental misspeaking and deliberate lies. Between an honest mistake and a swindle. Between saying you love the rules while you break them.

As I sat there on my bed, a wise Bible teacher and writer came in and sat beside me. "You know, rules are necessary." She smiled. "But we don't always have to enforce them."

God had the last word in the rule-breaking incident. By afternoon, those in charge had forgotten their threat. I taught my classes knowing God—he or she or both or neither—had intervened. I was glad that I'd decided to stay.

"It is the beginning of wisdom when you recognize that the best you can do is choose which rules you want to live by, and it's persistent and aggravated imbecility to pretend you can live without any."

—Wallace Stegner

When You Keep Your Palms Open

I will give you a new heart and put a new spirit in you; I will remove from you your heart of stone and give you a heart of flesh.
—Ezekiel 36:26

In the middle of the night, I got up to use the bathroom. I sat down and fell into the bowl. I was surprised, but as I walked back to bed, I caught sight of my dear ex-Marine husband, standing at the garage door, smoking a cigarette. I was more than a bit irritated.

Instead of wisely crawling under the covers, I marched up to him. With my eyes full of sleep and my hand on my hip, I said, "You left the seat up. Wanna know how I know this?"

He hid the cig, looking like a guilty child. I pulled out the sarcasm. "Don't bother to hide it. Why won't you quit?"

His eyes sparked defensively. "Stop telling me what to do." He put out the butt and stomped off to sleep on the sofa.

I stood there, fuming. But then, that still small voice invaded my thoughts. God let me know that I could have done things differently. The image of a shaking fist looped in my head. In being so right, I'd been wrong.

I don't remember ever shaking a fist at anyone, although I've certainly been angry enough to want to do just that. If my late husband left the toilet seat up or refused to stop smoking, for example. I let him know whenever I thought he was inconsiderate, whether of me or of his own well-being.

The Bible has a lot to say about righteousness. We, as Jesus followers, are to be reckoned as righteous in all our ways. Yet the Scriptures are much quieter when it comes to telling others if they aren't right. Prophets and Jesus Himself were criticized for spelling out the wrongs of their generations. As we try to live with the same regard for others as ourselves, we can get caught in a cycle of accusation and judgment.

Yet God gives us a blueprint for dealing with others' faux pas. Jesus says first we must get the log out of our own eyes before getting upset with others' splinters (Matthew 7:3-5). Elders are instructed to gently take aside wayward members if a course correction is needed (Galatians 6:1-2). Most of all, if we walk by the Spirit in love, we can approach others by keeping our palms open and face up, not clenched in a fist.

The next morning, I woke up on the brighter side of the bed. God had given me a new attitude. I apologized to my hubby and admitted that nagging at three a.m. was a poor way to convince him to stop smoking. I asked him to try to remember the toilet seat and promised to always look before I sit. I held out my open palms to invite a morning hug.

"The Golden Rule works. It really does. Treat people the way you want to be treated. Kindness begets kindness."

—Michael J. Silverstein

When Forgiveness Gets Easier

Then Peter came to Jesus and asked, "Lord, how many times shall I forgive my brother or sister who sins against me? Up to seven times?" Jesus answered, "I tell you, not seven times, but seventy-seven times.
—Matthew 18: 21-22

On Easter Sunday, my teenage son wouldn't look at me. I was dressed for church and still in shock. I'd walked outside to discover he'd taken the family car for a spin without permission. My heart hurt.

"I forgive you," I said.

He mumbled thanks. The moment felt awkward for both of us. He slunk away to his room.

I made it to church that Easter, even though my emotions still roiled with sadness and anger. He admitted his wrong, probably because he'd been caught pulling into the driveway. But my son had broken my trust, and although I forgave, the whole incident stuck in my throat like peanut butter with nothing to wash it down.

Nobody likes to admit they've been wrong. And nobody I know likes it when others refuse to admit they've wronged another. Forgiving and being forgiven are often hard to do and hard to receive. But Jesus doesn't let us off the hook.

Seventy times seven is a lot of forgiving.

Some interpret this passage as an ideal that we'll probably never attain. People are going to goof up, irritate us, or worse, harm us. If we say we forgive, yet let bitterness or resentment grow, it's not really forgiveness. Or is it?

I think God knows how difficult this forgiveness thing can be. Authentic forgiveness asks us to trust after trust has been torn. The journey back to trust is often long, full of switchbacks, and exhausting.

Maybe that's why Jesus asks us to be innocent as doves but wise as serpents (Matthew 10:16). If forgiveness leads to more harm, trust only leads to foolishness. And we must also be wise enough to determine where on the scale of wrongdoing the offense lies. God doesn't want us to freak out over petty differences, and God doesn't want us to ignore harmful or malevolent behavior either (Ezekiel 16:58). Forgiveness and consequences can exist at the same time as God demonstrates again and again throughout Scripture.

As parents, we must learn what appropriate consequences are best to retrain and restore trust. If a child spills the milk or forgets to empty the trash, we don't throw the kid into the outer darkness. When a child knows the rules and flaunts them defiantly, we set consequences to reinforce family values and rebuild trust.

My son faced consequences for his actions. But I forgave him—my love for him never wavered. After a while, trust returned. When my teenage son had my permission to borrow the car again, he made sure the windshield was clean, and the gas tank wasn't on empty. The more I concentrate on loving, the easier forgiveness becomes.

"We must develop and maintain the capacity to forgive. He who is devoid of the power to forgive is devoid of the power to love."
—Martin Luther King Jr.

When Gratitude is a Way of Life

Praise the Lord. Give thanks to the Lord, for
he is good; his love endures forever.
—Psalm 106:1

The first-time doctors sent me to the crippled children's hospital in Utah, I was nine. Doctors there promised to perform surgery on my paralyzed left arm and hand—surgery that would give me more functional use. If successful, that hand would have stronger fingers, a straightened wrist, and a working opposable thumb. My grandma gushed that I was so lucky.

As I boarded the plane in Phoenix, I was scared spitless, and I didn't know what surgery would be like. I was shaking inside when the pretty stewardess handed me the white paper airsickness bag. What nobody knew was that I didn't feel very lucky. And I sure wasn't grateful.

When I arrived at the hospital, my left wrist was painfully straightened and wrapped in a plaster cast. That was only the beginning of three long months of operations, homesickness, and trying to figure out why God was mad at me. I felt more like a guinea pig than a patient.

We can feel dumped upon at some point. We read Paul's directive to rejoice always and think, *easy for you to say*. We put on blinders so we don't have to compare ourselves with people who battle disasters, famine, disease, and war. There's always someone worse off, but guilty gratitude (because kids far away are starving) isn't true thankfulness, and deep down, we know it.

Cultivating authentic gratitude is hard, especially when you've grown up feeling entitled to a way of life. Back at that hospital, a charity-run organization, those in charge tried to level the field. Patients couldn't receive gifts or have so much as a stuffed animal sent from home. We couldn't wear our own clothes. Twice weekly, we chose ugly homemade outfits from a rack.

But one look at the other girls made me change my mind about gratitude. Many of them sported plaster casts that covered them from chins to toes. I was usually the only one who could walk unaided, Some of these kids couldn't sit up.

For three-and-half months, I fetched dropped items and carried bedpans when nurses were too busy. I might have stopped at guilty gratitude, only comparing my disability with others. But we were all lonely, homesick, and scared. We leaned on each other for comfort, laughter, and friendship.

On nights when some poor girl couldn't stop crying in pain, I'd reach under my pillow, where I stashed my little white King James Version Bible. I'd pray for the hurting, and I'd thank God that he wraps his arms around us all. That's the kind of gratitude I want to remember every day.

"When I started counting my blessings, my whole life turned around."

—Willie Nelson

part three

He Carried You Through Daily

Don't Look Down, Look Up!

Have I not commanded you? Be strong and courageous. Do not be afraid; do not be discouraged, for the Lord your God will be with you wherever you go."
—Joshua 1:9

The guide at the Grand Canyon said, "Whatever you do, don't look down." We were at the West Rim Skywalk, an overhang jutting out ten feet from the canyon's edge.

It had taken me so long to visit this place. My fear of heights had limited me before—I could barely ride an elevator without panicking. Fear overpowered my curiosity in other situations, too. Okay, I was often scared out of my mind.

I gripped the Skywalk railing, shuffling tiny steps. A man behind me bumped my elbow, and I nearly jumped out of my skin. "Don't look down." I shut my eyes.

The first and last time I tried ice skating was a bust, too. I was scared, and my ankles were weak, but my husband said my fears were silly. With my skates laced tight enough to cut off circulation, I hugged the rail while my husband glided circles around me. Even moving an inch buckled my ankles. I was afraid of falling, afraid I'd fail. Just plain afraid.

As we try to grow closer to God, fear often gets in the way. Throughout Scripture, God tells us not to be afraid. But life isn't easy, and there are plenty of things to be fearful about. Just about everybody worries about safety, security, belonging, and love. Worry leads to anxiety, and if we let fears take over, we're stuck in a perpetual fight or flight stance.

I've learned that in life there are no guarantees, except one. The God who created everything loves each and every one of us (John 3:16). From sinful soul to living saint, God is crazy about you and me—and yes, even that one guy who upsets you on the daily.

God's love is more than an idea. Jesus wants to crawl into our hearts and set up camp, no matter what we're facing (Revelation 3:20). When we can't go on, the Lord picks us up. He doesn't complain that we're too heavy. No, he claims the yoke is easy, the burden light (Matthew 11:30).

The more we hand off those fears and allow Jesus to carry us, the more hope can expand. Hope isn't just crossing fingers for a certain outcome or praying to be lifted out of trouble. The more we relax into the Everlasting arms, the more hope becomes our attitude toward all of life—scary places included.

I'm still a terrible ice skater, and I avoid rooftops. Yet whenever I think of running from my fears, Jesus beckons me to trust that he'll always carry me through whatever high or low spot I face.

As I stood on that platform, hanging over the Grand Canyon, I shook, trying not to look down. God seemed to whisper, "Look up!" I laughed and took in the magnificent sky's beautiful colors.

"The best way out is always through."
—Robert Frost

When Jesus Carries You Through Every Single Day

Keep your lives free from the love of money and be content with what you have, because God has said, "Never will I leave you; never will I forsake you."
—Hebrews 13:5

Our phone conversation had ended an hour ago, well past my bedtime. My adult daughter, a running enthusiast, was giving me her weekend itinerary for running a race in another city. She promised to check in frequently.

But I couldn't sleep. Before I ended the call, I'd forgotten to tell my daughter, "I love you."

Whenever my grown kids, grands, dads, or husband is ready to hang up the phone, we end the call with, "I love you."

Forgetting that ending felt terrible as I lay there stewing. It was only a ritual, but I tossed and turned, debating whether to phone her again. I glanced at the clock—three a.m. No way would I interrupt her sleep the night before her big race.

As we walk with God, guilt can creep in for all sorts of reasons. Maybe we let a spat with a loved one go unresolved. Maybe we became frustrated with someone and spoke unkindly. We accidentally cut off the car behind us. One time, I drove home from the grocery store before I realized I'd forgotten to pay for an item on the cart's bottom rack.

In these situations, a little guilt or what some call *conviction* helps us straighten out when we act a bit too human. God wants us to course-correct on our own (I John 1:9). But if we pile false guilt on ourselves or others—saying we're too this or that, not enough of something else—Jesus pulls us into his arms and whispers, "I'm here, loving you and everybody. No matter what."

As I journey toward a deeper walk with God, I spot Jesus everywhere. Whether it's comfort, encouragement, or mercy, the Lord never tires of doing the heavy lifting. Here's Jesus reflected in a kind stranger's face. There's Jesus offering a shoulder to cry on. He talks me out of my snippy mood, my open-mouth-insert-foot moment, my stubborn refusal to see another viewpoint.

Even on the worst days of my life, Jesus stays close, soothing my wounds, blasting away fear, and bolstering hope. Whether I forgot to say, "I love you" or I'm faced with life or death, Jesus is there like a favorite soft shirt that also happens to be the Lord of all.

First thing the next morning, I dialed my daughter's phone to apologize for missing our traditional goodbye. "I love you," I said as Jesus boosted me over my guilty sadness. I thought I heard him say, "I love you too. No matter what."

"We may ignore, but we can nowhere evade the presence of God. The world is crowded with Him. He walks everywhere incognito."

—C. S. Lewis

When the Miracle is Late

The Lord is not slow in keeping his promise, as some understand slowness. Instead, he is patient with you, not wanting anyone to perish, but everyone to come to repentance.
—II Peter 3:9

For many years, I prayed for my sons who struggled with addiction and mental illness. I genuinely believed that God could cure my three boys of their substance use. I searched endlessly for some program, approach, or prayer that would heal them.

The healing miracle I wanted, needed, was desperate for, always felt elusive. I tried to change them, and failing that, tried to change myself. If I was enabling, people said I had to get tough. If I was codependent, I had to separate myself from their problems. Go to meetings. Believe that God could heal and pray my heart out.

But the miracle was late.

I couldn't save my adult children. And maybe God either wasn't interested, or else God was trying to tell me I was wrong about all of this.

I felt worse than a failure. When we care about others, love can hurt. When someone we love has substance use problems, gets a terrible diagnosis, or betrays us, we feel helpless. If things stay the same for too long, we can become hopeless, too.

We try everything from shunning and shaming to praying for miracles while we suffer along with the person with addiction. We learn about this method, throw money at that program, and sometimes, we cut off relationships. We pray for a miracle healing with all our hearts.

And still, the miracle is late. One person overdoses. Another dies of an awful disease. An accident takes another That betrayal gets turned around, and now you're the bad guy. Where's God's miracle?

The only way I was able to maintain hope for my sons was by praying in a different way. Instead of an instantaneous healing, I prayed for God's love to flood their being. I changed what I could about myself—swapping judgment and disgust for love and forgiveness. And I gave them back into God's hands, where God can carry *them* through even this. I've had to accept that they may never change to my liking. Maybe they'll keep on using substances.

But their substance abuse is not an excuse to stop loving them as Jesus loves. In fact, when we let go of our expectations or outcomes, evidence shows that more people with addiction recover with support than with punishment. I lovingly draw boundaries to encourage natural consequences and to keep my values intact.

I like what Biblical scholar Fr. Richard Rohr said of Jesus: Jesus didn't so much love people once they changed. He loved them so that they *could* change.

As a disabled/paralyzed woman, I've learned that sometimes the miracle I get isn't the one I prayed for. I still pray for my sons, and one has since actually laid down his drug of choice. But I don't try to tell God exactly what the miracle should look like. That's a miracle in itself.

"True faith does not so much attempt to manipulate God to do our will as it does to position us to do his will."
—Philip Yancey

When Suffering Equals Rejoicing

Now if we are children, then we are heirs—heirs of God and co-heirs with Christ, if indeed we share in his sufferings in order that we may also share in his glory.
—Romans 8:17

My son was in the middle of a rant, no doubt fueled by drug psychosis. Flecks of foamy spittle lined his lips, and his eyes were black holes. He'd already been up for days and kept spouting gibberish. But no matter what I did, he stopped every few moments and accused me of not listening or of interrupting him.

My heart sped up, and fear tinged the edges of my thoughts. I was determined to stay calm. I'd seen this movie before. Silently, I prayed and kept my expression impassive. At what point would I flee or call someone to intervene?

I'd want the local crisis van, not the police. My son has been mentally ill since early childhood but has never been violent. Like many mentally ill people, he self-medicated. And here we were, decades later, still dealing with calamity.

While you may not have the same troubles to cope with, we all suffer. Whether it's health, a loved one's decline, financial woes, or any number of other horrible things, suffering seems baked into our existence. Nobody I know loves the verses where Paul tells us to rejoice in our sufferings. I, for one, don't want to go to Paul's prison to find out if I can *rejoice and again I say rejoice* (Philippians 4:4). If we're honest, we say suffering in any way really stinks. So how come Paul spends so much time on suffering while rejoicing?

I guess that Jesus kicks it off by saying *in this world you will have trouble.* If we can't avoid suffering, what do we do about it?

I don't mind if you complain. We both hate to suffer. Usually, hindsight is the only way we can lift our suffering heads long enough to rejoice for even a minute. But look at the way the loved one whose cancer has returned faces it compared to the first time. A little girl I know is battling aggressive cancer for the umpteenth time. She cries and hates the pain and fatigue. But she still says God is good. She still hates to suffer, but she already knows what lies ahead. There's a calm and resolute attitude that wasn't there before. She's rejoicing at God's goodness even as life hands her deep-fried suffering on a stick.

Like the girl, when my son gets psychotic, I'm no longer afraid. I can help guide him to a calmer state if I remain stoic and have a plan in place. As I listened to him rant, I mentally prayed that God's love would overcome whatever was tormenting him.

He eventually wound down, sat at the table, and fell asleep. I had to rejoice.

"A setback is a setup for a comeback."
—T.D. Jakes

When Happiness is in the Middle of the Disaster

I am not saying this because I am in need, for I have learned to be content whatever the circumstances.
—Philippians 4:11

A few years ago, a late summer wildfire consumed a nearby community. An entire town on the beautiful Mackenzie River burned to the ground.

I didn't live there, but the sky above my area turned bright orange and rained ash for days. The folks who lived there lost everything.

Floods in Texas and New Mexico. Fires in Los Angeles. Hurricanes and tornadoes. Haboobs in the desert communities. These weather events devastate areas and uproot lives. The choices people make or governmental mistakes can wreak havoc through wars or hubris.

My biggest personal disasters have been either foolish mistakes I made or deaths I couldn't control. I've been pretty sheltered—I've never missed a meal except to diet. Although my disasters can't compare to an earthquake or a wildfire, they felt like a tsunami to me.

Hindsight might not help whatever disaster occurred, but it does help build wisdom. If we've had to flee rising flash flood waters, we know to always be prepared to dash away. Receiving a devastating diagnosis and discovering ways to cope, adapt, and make daily life workable is a hard-earned form of wisdom. Losing a home in a financial crisis teaches us to I build a nest egg against future disasters.

In my estimation, wisdom learned from difficult experiences helps us hope. And of course, hope doesn't disappoint. With God's hope, we learn to see the smallest joys and the quiet ways he helps us bear our sorrow. He has placed them all around us—in the wren's song, the whisper of leaves, even in the homely beauty of a toad lifting its voice. We touch the earth, breathe the rain, and taste the miracle of honey fashioned by God's faithful bees.

Sometimes happiness comes from another person. A stranger's smile, thanks murmured when something lost is returned, a child twirling in the grass. These and more can remind us that life is beautiful and terrible and made by a loving God who delights in our happiness.

The people who lost everything in the Holiday Farm fire had every reason to be sad, mad, and point blaming fingers. But many of them chose, in the middle of their disastrous calamity, to help others.

They knew the secret to happiness in the middle of disaster. When the fire or the water or the wind tries to destroy our positive outlook, it's okay to go ahead and wail. Really. But then look around and see who needs our help. Take a few moments to pray and appreciate the awe-inspiring things of God's creation. Then we roll up our sleeves and help Jesus carry others as he carries us.

"There is a light that shines in the darkness, which is only visible there."

—Barbara Brown Taylor

When You Love an Ungrateful Meanie

But love your enemies, do good to them, and lend to them without expecting to get anything back. Then your reward will be great, and you will be children of the Most High, because he is kind to the ungrateful and wicked.
—Luke 6:35

I once dated a man who said he loved me even though my left arm is paralyzed. But he criticized my every move and demanded to know where I was at all times.

Red flags waved, but I overlooked them. After all, everybody makes mistakes. He was an ex-Marine and veteran of Vietnam War. I justified his sharp-edged comments by telling myself he must have PTSD (Post-Traumatic-Stress-Disorder).

As time went on, he stepped up his sarcastic and downright mean remarks about my figure and my intelligence. I thought I could sweeten him up with loving words and deeds. Of course, it was never enough.

I tried to make him love me as much as I thought I loved him. He didn't even say thank you when I mended his shirts or cooked a meal. I accepted the verbal abuse until one evening, I'd had enough. "Maybe we should see other people."

"Who'd want a cripple like you?" He slapped my face. "You have to swim in a circle."

I hope few of us experience that level of abuse. Yet we've known people who constantly build themselves up by tearing others down. People who don't bother to build relationships unless there's something for them to gain. Ungrateful meanies.

Too often, these meanies are in our own families. We can try to distance ourselves from grumpy Uncle Fred or nod along politely as Aunt Harriet lists everything that's wrong with us and our world. Sometimes we find ourselves hurt and furious with our own parents or children. Whether it's over politics, an inheritance, or family disagreements, loving an ungrateful meanie feels impossible.

What about turn the other cheek? Love people who now seem like enemies? Wow, Jesus, that's a really tall order. All through history, loved ones have plotted against each other or tried to get even.

It's easy to point a finger and remind someone that "It is mine to avenge; I will repay," says the Lord," Romans 12:19. But does the Lord know how bad it is? My ungrateful meanie is worse than anyone else's. What does God want from us, anyway?

God's answer is the only answer. Keep loving. Don't necessarily give that person extra ammo to abuse us, but don't allow hate to gain a foothold in our hearts. If we let ourselves be consumed by revenge, we diminish Spirit-led love. We fill our own hearts with bitter resentment. Resentment can lead to feuds, even wars.

I said goodbye to that guy, and suddenly a great weight lifted from my shoulders. I was free to see him as God saw him—a person who, in rejecting true love, had shrunk his own heart into a dried-up prune. I could love him and let God's goodness swim circles around him.

"Ingratitude is always a kind of weakness. I have never known men of ability to be ungrateful."
—Johann Wolfgang von Goethe

When You're Smothered in Love

Love is patient, love is kind. It does not envy,
it does not boast, it is not proud.
—I Corinthians 13:4

When I first met my late husband Brad, he fell head over heels in love with me. I liked him too but wanted to get to know him first. I was on summer vacation in San Diego and would soon return Arizona and my job teaching art to elementary school kids.

My guy treated me as if I were some sort of goddess. He fawned over me. I liked him more each day but became annoyed at his smothering ways.

I hadn't been raised in a family where hugging or other shows of affection were common. When he rubbed my shoulders or my feet, I tried hard not to recoil. That much touching was almost painful for me. I finally confessed that I wasn't comfortable with so much closeness.

Sometimes, loved ones don't realize they're smothering, and other times, they're well-aware. Mothers often want to know where their children are at all times. Fathers worry during the teenage years and, long after those years have passed, may continue to insert themselves into areas where independence and confidence have already taken root. Loving relationships can slip out of balance, reaching a point where one partner must pull back to regain equilibrium.

When the other person feels hurt or rejected, we can offer reassurance while still establishing reasonable boundaries for ourselves. But when that response turns aggressive or abusive, it becomes necessary to ask whether control—not love—was the true aim.

All through Scripture, God models authentic love. God forgives, has mercy, and loves when we don't deserve a break. Jesus shows us what real love looks like, and I Corinthians 13 spells out love's attributes.

We can be seduced by the illusion of love if we've never experienced God's ways of loving us. Sometimes we end up either smothering or being smothered by another person. To cut through phony love, watch what people do more than what they say.

Do their actions reflect respect and dignity? Does the person respect and honor boundaries?

Conversely, are we respecting the boundaries of others? If asked to refrain from some behavior, do we value that person enough to try to change? Relationships often endure because of the loving respect each person has for the other.

Thankfully, my guy listened to my words and stopped being so touchy-feely. I learned how to become less stingy with affection and enjoy hugs. With decades of practice, we worked out loving without smothering. I'm still working on hugging others and loving hugs. Two different people came together and our marriage lasted forty-seven years.

"The fear is suffocating, terrorizing, and I want the remedy, and it is trust. Trust is everything."
—Ann Voskamp

When You're Still a Doubter

Then he said to Thomas, "Put your finger here; see my hands. Reach out your hand and put it into my side. Stop doubting and believe."
—John 20:27

My adoptive dad, Jack, used to tell me to "do as I say, not as I do." Growing up, I felt as if he was dangling some sort of adult privilege in front of me like a carrot. But if I dared to question his judgments, the stick came out pretty fast.

Not a literal stick, mind you. But his promise that one day I too would have all the answers often devolved into verbal threats and the awful specter of being grounded until I was ninety-five. By the time I went to college, I could laugh at all that. He was a big old softie under that gruff exterior. But as a youngster, I was afraid to doubt.

I admit that I'm skeptical. I need to see facts, evidence, or some sort of validation before I buy into a theory or an offer. In my Christian life, I've been a doubter too. I ask questions. I follow logic. I simply can't check my brain at the sanctuary door.

Intuition tells me to doubt if someone in a position over me is only trying to make themselves look better. My heart—which I aim to keep filled with Jesus' love—pings if corruption or falsehoods are foisted on me or others—especially the ones with little power. The ones Jesus called the least of these.

If we're honest, we've all doubted at one time or another. An old meme from the 80s—God said it, I believe it, that settles it—takes away our free will capacity to love, to serve, to never question. If we can't doubt, we may end up walking away.

Poor Thomas is often held up as the prime doubter-in-chief. Jesus told him to quit doubting and believe. Yet somehow, I can't see how Jesus meant *never question any Biblical interpretation or pastoral edict.* To do so would negate love in so many instances. Jesus instructs us to be as shrewd as serpents and as gentle as doves (Matthew 10:16). Our Lord's life and teaching revealed that love stands at the center of God's kingdom. He invited us to love God, to love our neighbors, and to practice compassion and peace—not as ideals, but as daily acts of faith.

A healthy doubt seeks to know more about the mystery of God. Healthy doubt allows for questions, skeptical inquiries, and even challenges. Our God is big enough to weather our doubts and to transform us as we connect our hearts to God's heart.

In my life, the more questions I ask, the deeper I fall in love with the Author of Love. I want to be able to worship and serve not because somebody says I should, but because that's what love does—it gives itself away.

"Doubt is the beginning, not the end, of wisdom."
—George Iles

When the Road is Too Darn Long

Therefore, since we are surrounded by such a great cloud of witnesses, let us throw off everything that hinders and the sin that so easily entangles. And let us run with perseverance the race marked out for us,
—Hebrews 12:1

After my husband of forty-seven years passed away from a massive stroke, I felt numb. Three weeks before Christmas, I didn't feel much of anything. Although I knew he was with God now, my faith teetered, and I didn't care if I celebrated Christ's birth or not.

Instead, I kept coming back to the same questions: What would life be like for me as a widow? Could I even go on as a Christian?

I wish I could say I never once doubted. But circumstances weren't ideal financially—we'd lost the only home we'd owned, and his life insurance hadn't been mature enough to pay out in full. I had two grown, live-in sons with serious problems that prevented them from working. Rents were skyrocketing everywhere. Would we end up homeless like so many unfortunate Americans?

Too many life events can make it hard for good people to be optimistic—people lose jobs, homes, or loved ones. Relationships fail. Diseases or disasters rob us of a decent life. The road back to any sort of stability or safety seems impossibly long.

And yet, God says, "Fear not."

During times when we just can't go on, God tells us not to be afraid? How can I *not* quake in my boots as I'm losing my life's partner or my child or my job or my house?

The only way I can keep walking that long road is to know that Jesus carries me through.

In the deepest recesses of my heart, I sense that the Lord is right there beside me, offering wisdom, comfort, and hope. Being carried by God through anything and everything is different than believing I'm saved or knowing *about* the Lord. Being carried by God means that although I wish (and pray with every fiber of my being) to be removed from whatever evil has befallen, Jesus Himself hefts me up on His shoulder, where I rest like a beloved lamb.

When God carries us, we can better deal with doubts. We can begin to face those ugly fears and even laugh at them. We may even relax our worries about how in God's good name we'll ever survive what's happening.

None of this is easy, of course. But Brother Lawrence from the seventeenth century left some good advice. Practice being in God's presence every day, all day, in good times and horrid times. Repeat some Scripture or a saying that gives peace and courage. Remember our love for God. And that God loves us.

The road to being a widow is long. But my sidekick Jesus has strong arms to boost faith and courage and hope.

"It's not whether you get knocked down,
it's whether you get back up."
—Vince Lombardi

When it's Hard to Forgive

If we confess our sins, he is faithful and just and will forgive us our sins and purify us from all unrighteousness.
—I John 1:9

I stood over my two sons. "Say you're sorry!" I commanded the ten-year-old. "Forgive your brother," I said to the eight-year-old.

Both boys crossed their arms and shot mean looks at each other.

"Go on," I said. "I'm waiting."

The two of them played like brothers, pulled pranks like brothers, and sometimes fought like siblings do. That summer afternoon, what began as a joke, according to the older one, had blown up into a yelling match. I had to restrain their urges to pummel each other. And now, neither boy was willing to patch things up.

My younger son had tears in his eyes. "I'm never playing with him again."

My oldest muttered, "Don't be a baby."

I stood between them, trying to cool hot tempers so they could think about their impulsive actions.

I wish I could say that *I'm* able to easily forgive. Often, I'll give a shallow apology or say, "*de nada*," but true forgiveness can be much harder for most of us—especially if the infraction is more serious than a childhood spat. If we're hurt by someone we care about—trust is broken over lies or cheating, backstabbing, or embezzling. We find that Mount Forgiveness is very tall and very steep.

If we're the one who needs forgiving, guilty shame can eat away at our relationships, our self-esteem, and the ability to come to God with the messes we've made. I used to worry that God was waiting for me to make a mistake. After all, I'm human and I've felt tempted like everyone else. Tempted to lie, cheat—heck, once I even stole a tube of lipstick from a drugstore. Impulsive enough to say hurtful things or to be passive-aggressive. In every case, I've prayed for forgiveness and release from that shame.

To my joyful surprise, God has been more than willing to forgive me for sins big and small. One look through the book of Isaiah or any of Jesus' words reassures me that if I confess my sin, God won't even remember what I did wrong. The Son of God forgave those who crucified him. God's generous forgiveness helps me learn to forgive and be forgiven even when it's hard.

My sons still wanted to be mad even after I forced them to make up. I've certainly had to do forgiveness in little chunks when an issue sticks in my craw. Sometimes deep hurts take years to heal. God pours out extra love to help carry us to the top of Mt. Forgive, and God smiles when we have to stop and rest before going any farther.

My boys took all day to reach forgiveness. Later that night, I heard them whispering from their beds. They were brothers again.

"Forgiveness is the fragrance that the violet sheds on the heel that has crushed it."

— Mark Twain

When You Feel Trapped

My eyes are ever on the Lord, for only he
will release my feet from the snare.
—Psalm 25:15

On a floating trip down Arizona's Verde River, my inner tube bumped over a small waterfall and flipped. I went about six feet underwater. As I tried to surface, the water pressure kept churning and holding me down. For what felt like eternity, I kept paddling toward the light.

I'm pretty claustrophobic—I can't stand to be in a tight or crowded space. I even have to sleep with my sleeping bag unzipped, so I can keep my feet free. Feeling as if I was drowning was as scary as being trapped in an elevator.

Those physical feelings of being trapped can't compare with the feelings of emotional entrapment. If you've ever felt trapped in a relationship, a job, or a situation, you know that indecision, guilt, and feeling trapped can trigger a fight or flight response. Especially in cases where you feel less powerful than someone or something, feeling trapped gnaws at your well-being.

A controlling spouse, parent, or boss often makes it hard to break away, even harder to assert one's own agency. And if the person or entity doing the controlling claims a Scriptural privilege, we can feel as if even God wants us trapped.

That's a lie.

Sometimes we feel trapped by nature or by people, but a loving God doesn't work that way. No, God wants to free us from all the snares life throws around us (Psalm 141: 9). Like a kind sailor who cuts away tangled nets from a frightened seal or dolphin, God wants us free to live and love without fear.

When we feel trapped in a relationship, fear of loss, abandonment, or change keeps us anchored in unhealthy situations. What if I'm alone? What if no one will ever love me? What if I'm a failure? By following Jesus' example, we can learn to make decisions in love without resorting to bitterness, revenge, or violence. We can rest in God's love.

In our prayer closet, we can talk things over with God. Make lists of pros and cons if we need to. Study Scripture to gain wisdom, speak with trusted confidantes. We might be able to unravel an unhealthy relationship, find a new job, separate in love from whatever pins us down.

Society says, "do unto others before they do to you." But Jesus lifts the Golden Rule, helping us love others as ourselves. When the walls close in, we can let Jesus carry us back across our dilemma to the river of life.

As I held my breath underwater that day on the Verde River, I had a feeling of calm that I can't explain. Jesus was somehow there with me. I finally surfaced, thanking God, with a peace that passed understanding.

"We can't be trapped by fear. Lives lived within such walls are just slower deaths."

—Mark Lawrence

When Your Relationships Get Rocky

"Salt is good, but if it loses its saltiness, how can you make it salty again? Have salt among yourselves and be at peace with each other."
—Mark 9:50

If only I'd kept my big mouth shut. I'd had a little falling out with a friend who was a writing partner and old enough to be my mother. As we sifted through the proofs of a book we wrote together, we disagreed about something in the manuscript. She became irate and yelled at me.

I don't remember why we disagreed. But she couldn't let it go. She berated me over what she regarded as a terrible mistake. I felt guilty, and worried that I'd ruined a beautiful friendship.

My tongue gets me into trouble, and when it's on fire as the Book of James says, it's hard to restore a relationship. I've learned some tough lessons whenever my relationships—spouse, children, parents, friends—get rocky. We endanger how we interact with others by stuff we say or don't say. In the split second we have to answer for ourselves, we choose whether to be real or whether to keep up appearances.

Sometimes, that fiery tongue spills over into wrong actions that further separate us from our trusted relationships. But no matter why a relationship grows bumpy, God always seems to have the same answer: love.

Love is the only way we can arrive at forgiveness or to be honest enough to receive it. As long as we insist on being right, on being innocent, or on only seeing things from our own perspective, God has a much harder time working with us. A rocky relationship usually means trust is somehow broken. Broken trust prevents genuine love from abiding or enduring all things (1 Corinthians 13:7).

In the most serious cases, where physical, mental, or emotional danger is present, God can help us love others from a distance. While Jesus says we're to be at peace with others, it doesn't mean they can simply stomp over us in ways that rob us of our dignity and agency or worse.

Still, when a relationship slips off the rails, we can evaluate whether it's a healthy one to patch up. If we value that person's presence in our lives, we can soften our hearts and relax our stiff necks the same way God shows us mercy. In a stand-off, we can decide to love the other person even though we think they're wrong. We can let go of the need to be right for the sake of love.

Later, when my friend met me at a café, I worried I'd need to break off our friendship. But as we sat there, a tear rolled down my face. She stopped attacking me and apologized for her behavior. We both thanked God. Jesus had carried us both to a place where love could have the last word.

"There is no reconciliation until you recognize the dignity of the other, until you see their view- you have to enter into the pain of the people. You've got to feel their need."

—John M. Perkins

When You Really Need Courage

Be strong and courageous. Do not be afraid or terrified because of them, for the Lord your God goes with you; he will never leave you nor forsake you."
—Deuteronomy 31:6

At age nine, I arrived in a strange city and state, far away from my family. Before I boarded the plane alone, my grandmother encouraged me to be brave. "You'll be home in no time," she said. "Doctors are going to fix your arm to make it work better." She handed me a white leather-bound Bible, with a zipper and KJV stamped in gold.

At the children's hospital, I followed a nurse to the bathroom. I bathed, and then she put my clothing in a box and handed me clothes to wear. She tried to put my white Bible into the box too, but I held it behind my back. She sighed, and I followed her to another room.

I've never thought of myself as especially brave. Sure, I can remove a spider. I can speak in front of an audience and drive in big-city rush hour traffic.

But I can't imagine being a wartime soldier like my late husband, the Marine. Or standing up against anything that's life or death—like being exiled or enslaved like the Israelites. Many of us have a difficult time pushing back against someone or something that has real power over us.

If we somehow don't act with bravery, we tend to blame ourselves. I hold an unflattering self-image in cases when I have twenty-twenty hindsight. It's easy to beat myself up after the crisis has passed.

And yet, we also tend to respond to emergencies with courage. We run into a burning building to save a person or even a pet. We give CPR and hold a stranger's hands until the paramedics arrive. We rise to the occasion, whether it's a natural disaster or a car crash.

Until our mettle is tested, we often don't know how brave we can be. Maybe we must learn to be brave.

Courage grows when we remember that we're never alone. David stepped onto the battlefield fortified by a courage rooted in God. Peter, after denying Jesus, discovered that same courage rekindled within him.

Jesus had been there with Peter all along. And that's the thing about the scary things we face—he will never leave or forsake us. Ever. If we feel cowardly or not up to the task, Jesus gladly carries us to a place where our feet of clay can become wills of steel. With God at our side, we can be as strong and courageous as the Scripture commands.

I stayed in that hospital for three long months, underwent two major surgeries, and didn't see my family for Christmas. I battled loneliness and fear. But every night I prayed and reached under my pillow for my little white Bible so Jesus could carry me to morning. And he always did.

"Courage is what it takes to stand up and speak; courage is also what it takes to sit down and listen."

—Winston Churchill

When the Armor of God Feels Too Big

Therefore, put on the full armor of God, so that when the day of evil comes, you may be able to stand your ground, and after you have done everything, to stand.
—Ephesians 6:13

When my four kids were little, I spent a lot of time buckling them in and out of car seats. They'd wriggle and complain. But I'd tell them that God was making sure they were safe.

I've gone through times when every day feels pretty evil in a ho-hum kind of way. The job I thought was so dreamy turns out to be a trudge through repetitive tasks and dull routines. The years when kids overwhelmed me every single minute. The dry spells of my forty-seven-year marriage.

With every crisis, mundane or urgent, I tried to put on the armor of God. And many times, it's been too big and way too heavy.

We who place our trust in God often find ourselves strapping on armor to stand against all the crud that life throws at us. And for too many, God's armor makes us look like a kid playing dress-up. The Helmet of Salvation slips down over our eyes. Truth chafes our thighs. The Breastplate of Righteousness strains against our own sense of indignation and self-righteousness. The Gospel of Peace pinches our toes. We find the Shield of Faith almost too heavy to lift, and if the Spirit's Sword should slip, watch out.

No matter the situation, all these weapons are easier to talk about than actually wield. I always feel nervous and clumsy, fearing that none of the armor will fit. Even worse, I'm afraid I won't have the first clue in battling the evil opponent.

But God gives us a clue. The weapon of choice is not just any sword. The Spirit forges steel that is full of wisdom and full of grace and mercy. God seems to say that if we lead with the Sword of the Spirit, we won't be so tempted to get revenge or provoke a full-blown war.

The remainder of the armor is designed more for protection than for defeating an adversary. Jesus tells us we must be shrewd as snakes and as innocent as doves. I take it to mean that the Holy Spirit knows better than I do how to deal with whatever I'm up against.

Thankfully, God doesn't send us out there naked. With salvation, truth, righteousness, peace, and a Holy Spirit sidekick, we're equipped to stand against evil. The armor of God might be a few sizes too big, but with that Sword leading the way, we can feel confident to face the trials and general awfulness that life can bring.

I once thought that putting on the armor meant that God was sending me out like David facing Goliath. I worried that with one blow, I'd be toast. But God only wants us to strap into holy car seats, with a five-point harness and plenty of padding.

The battlefield for spiritual warfare is primarily in your thought life (2 Corinthians 10:4-5).

—Rick Warren

When You Forget that God Carries You

Are not two sparrows sold for a penny? Yet not one of them will fall to the ground outside your Father's care.
—Matthew 10:29

I leaned against my mini-trampoline, ready to cry along with my three-month-old twins. I'd been feeding and changing and burping and soothing these premature babies for the past hour and a half. The trampoline was my bright idea for jostling them to sleep. It hadn't worked.

My two older boys, ages seven and nearly four, would be home from school in a few hours. Every day, I raced to complete household chores while the twins napped. Except getting them to nap seemed almost impossible. The doctor had told me that until they gained more weight, the babies would be fussy.

Once my rambunctious boys were home, the house was too noisy for the babies to sleep. I'd tried taking them for stroller walks and car rides, but they screamed louder. We were three months into the adventure, and my own lack of sleep threatened to make me crazy.

Not all of us are parents, but when we find ourselves between proverbial rocks and hard spots, it's easy to lose sight of God in our midst. We pray for help, and if the answer isn't swift or obvious, we think God must be too busy to see to our needs.

At one time or another, we feel as if God needs hearing aids. We send out SOS prayers, and it's natural to beg God to lift away whatever we're up against. If we hear little except our own heartbeats, we conclude that we're on our own. God isn't coming to rescue us from the tough thing we face—maybe God even forgot about us.

But it's worth remembering that even God's Son had that same thought. As he hung on the cross, Jesus cried out, "My God, why have you forsaken me?" That moment of the Passion assures me that Jesus was both fully divine and fully human. If he could be so distraught as to think he'd been abandoned, we humans don't have to be ashamed for thinking we just didn't get a God appointment. Saint Paul, too, complained about that thorn that God wouldn't remove.

Both examples show that although God doesn't always lift us out of difficulty, God still carries us through whatever we're battling. Despite Jesus' agony and feelings of loneliness, he also told the thief at his right that he would see paradise. Paul was able to rejoice, not *for* all things, but *in* all things. They knew that God was there with them, and that thorny sides and horrific crosses couldn't separate them from the God of love.

And no matter what, God says the same thing to every one of us: That God will never leave us nor forsake us. That we are precious in God's sight. That God gladly will carry us through whatever awful thing comes.

I cradled my two tinies as I leaned against the trampoline, praying and telling the babes how much they were loved. The next thing I knew, my older sons were shaking me awake. The babies and I had drifted off to sleep for a much-needed nap. As I carried the twins to change them, I smiled. God was carrying me, too.

"It is during our darkest moments that we must focus to see the light."
—Aristotle Onassis

When Stress Eats You Alive

"Therefore, I tell you, do not worry about your life, what you will eat or drink; or about your body, what you will wear. Is not life more than food, and the body more than clothes?
—Matthew 6:25

The headache pounded, throbbed, and made my stomach churn. Lying down in a dark room didn't help. Medications relieved the pain for only a few minutes before it came roaring back. The migraine lasted for days.

The doctor said I needed to reduce my stress level.

I ran through my collective responsibilities. I was responsible for my four school-age children, and I was chief cook and bottle washer for them and my husband.

But in this day and age, two incomes were necessary. I also ran an in-home childcare business. Five days a week, from dawn until dusk, I cared for five or six kids aged three to five.

Where could I reduce stress?

Stress is blamed for everything from headaches to insomnia. We feel as if we're hamsters on a very fast wheel, trying to keep up. We feel pulled in a thousand directions and then feel guilty when we can't do it all.

Many of us wish we could slow down and just enjoy life. But obligations and responsibilities never seem to take a break. Our insides gnaw at us, and we're always exhausted. We try our best every day, and it isn't enough.

When Jesus reminds us that lilies don't seem to toil and we aren't supposed to worry, it's tempting to laugh. *You don't live in the twenty-first century, dear Lord.* Yet the God of love stands firm. *Concentrate on living instead of stressing,* Jesus says (John 10:10).

When the walls close in and we're ready to scream, how can we trade stress for the peace that passes understanding? Jesus gives us a strong hint. His examples come from nature: lilies and birds and parts of creation that don't punch a time clock.

If we replace even a sliver of anxiety and worry with a moment to marvel at the natural world, stress can't compete. Watch the way the wind caresses the leaves of trees as it passes by or listen to birdsong when you're going to work at o-dark-thirty. Feel the rain on your face without fretting that your outfit is ruined. Study cloud formations, and maybe even wave at heaven.

If nature doesn't break the stress spell, complain. Let it all out—God's a really good listener. Vent and rage at all the ways stress is killing you, and while you're at it, cuddle up in God's arms of love. Breathe out stress as you breathe in peace.

I'm sure there are many holy ways to reduce stress from meditation to fasting to prayer. I often fight those headaches by taking a brisk walk, praying with every step. After I whine a while, I always hear that small still voice. *Don't forget, little one. I'll always carry you through, no matter what.* That's a real stressbuster.

"It's not the load that breaks you down. It's the way you carry it."
—Lou Holtz

When You're Still Lonely

Turn to me and be gracious to me, for
I am lonely and afflicted.
—Psalms 25:16

When I was a young teacher, I used to go to the local mall after school, just to watch people. I found it comforting to decompress after a long day answering to my students. I could be alone in a crowd.

Fast forward to my retirement years. About nine months after my husband passed away, I started to feel a widow's loneliness. Without a partner, I felt awkward, even around friends. I started thinking maybe I should volunteer, get out more, meet new people. Find a new crowd.

For the most part, I'm an introvert. Being with lots of people drains me. I didn't really want a new partner or relationship. I attended more church functions and did volunteer work. But no matter what I did, I still felt lonely.

People everywhere seem to share that feeling. Studies done after the COVID pandemic showed that even with smartphones and social media, we're lonelier than ever. Between doom scrolling, memes, and videos, technology that's supposed to connect us makes us feel lonely in a crowd. While your loneliness might look different from mine, we long for connection.

God wires us to want belonging, acceptance, and love. When we don't see evidence of enough of those things in our lives, it's as if we're starving. We need real food of affection. And our loving God knows it.

Where can we turn when there's no one to turn to? Scripture tells us again and again that God won't leave us or forsake us. If we feel lonely, having "God with skin on" is ideal. Believing in God's constant touch is harder when we feel abandoned by everyone. Harder, yes. But not impossible.

If we place our faith in a loving God, we can run to God when we stand alone. Jesus promises to always be with us, and he gave us the Holy Spirit to be a comfort and a help. Strengthened by God's love, those promises can get us through the long dark night.

In my life, loneliness is God's cue to remind me to reach out to others who are lonely or need help. Despite my introverted nature, if I focus on helping others—whether with hugs or help—I forget why I was lonely in the first place. I reach out to other recent widows or find ways to lend a hand to those who need it.

I'm no saint, but by loving others intentionally, God helps me overcome my feelings that no one cares. I may feel alone in a crowd, but with Jesus' arms carrying me, I can give away love to help somebody else feel less alone.

"We can all fight against loneliness by engaging in random acts of kindness."
—Gail Honeyman

When Your Child Suffers

Children are a heritage from the Lord,
offspring a reward from him.
—Psalm 127:3

Shortly after my elderly mother passed away, a friend's son in his early thirties died from an overdose. I remember gasping at the news. The guy, a decent mechanic, had worked on our cars and attended my church. He was also my son's friend.

Mother and son shared their first names and last initials. The kid was funny and full of life, and he loved his mom and dad and God, too. I loved the way his shaggy dark hair fell across mischievous, sparkling eyes.

Even so, he struggled with life. He had trouble settling into adulthood and self-medicated with different street drugs. My son, older than his friend, counseled him about the dangers of fentanyl. I don't believe that the friend knew his last dose was lethal.

Raising our children is one of the most important and rewarding jobs we'll ever do. We want our kids to have better lives than we had. When terrible things befall them—accidents, diseases, even addiction or mental illness—we hurt as much or more than if it happened to us.

They say losing a child is the worst pain imaginable. I haven't experienced this pain, and I pray my children will outlive me. Just witnessing several friends lose their precious kids to a premature death is agonizing enough. What can anyone say or do to soothe such an indescribable wound?

For those who've gone through such a tragedy, only God could ever fill such a gaping hole. Yet I wouldn't blame a parent if grieving included shaking one's fist at the heavens. Because grief is so individual, it's impossible to predict how I'd behave if my child suffered deeply.

But the God who loves us and will never leave or forsake us is also patient. God's mercy leaves room for anger and feelings of unfairness, even betrayal. Jesus went through agony as he went to the Cross. God understands this kind of anguish in a very personal way.

When we're done blaming and raging, when we only want a warm dark place to hide away, Jesus crawls in alongside, cradling us as we pour out our tears and fears.

If your child hurts, you hurt too. You want to stroke your child's hair and whisper that it'll be all right. You cry together, laugh together, love together. And if you open your heart, God comforts you in the same ways.

My friend is a mom who will never hear her son's laughter again. Nothing will ever fill that empty place. Yet God's love still permeates her whole being. Maybe she sometimes gets mad at the unfairness of his passing. But in between moments of sorrow and fury, the Holy Spirit holds her, and all those whose children hurt, in a tender and loving embrace.

"Even though you've experienced huge amounts of deep, inner healing, you may always carry an ache in your heart over your child's suffering."
—Dena Yohe

When a Loved One Has Addiction

The Lord is my rock, my fortress and my deliverer;
my God is my rock, in whom I take refuge, my shield
and the horn of my salvation, my stronghold.
—Psalm 18:2

One of my three sons was just thirteen when he was introduced to methamphetamine. At the time, I tried to rescue him in traditional ways. I went to Al-Anon. I read books and educated myself about the drug's effects. My husband and I tried tough love and the courts forced him into treatment.

Nothing worked.

We concentrated so much on him that we almost missed the fact that our other two sons struggled with alcohol. Shame and guilt plagued me. How on earth had we ended up with so much addiction? We tried so hard but love for our boys was never tough enough. And yet I could never stop loving them.

When someone we love has addiction issues, our culture has become brutal. Users are accused of being morally weak and are pushed away or punished. Their families are suspect too—labeled codependent or enabling unless they've turned their backs on the users. Add in the high percentage of users with mental health issues, and available resources become either expensive or unavailable.

Loved ones often feel caught in the middle of a system that is punitive and judgmental.

Parents and loved ones are expected to kick out or otherwise cut ties with the person struggling. We're often told that these people always lie, steal, and are manipulative. While a person with Substance Use Disorder will do or say almost anything for their next dose or drink, evidence-based studies have shown that more people recover with support than with punishment.

Slowly, attitudes and guidance are changing. These changes align with the way Jesus treated people. The Lord didn't demand that folks clean up their act before they could come to him. He loved sinners of all stripes. He said, "*Go now and leave your life of sin*," (John 8:11) but it wasn't a prerequisite.

Christ's love makes it possible for people to change. Those changes may come too slowly for a loved one's patience, but those with addiction have a better chance of recovery if they still have loved ones who can encourage them.

God leaves it up to each person to set limits or boundaries on their support. Maybe you don't give money, but you can always say, "I love you." Maybe you live apart, but you can pray and love the person as if they had cancer or a less stigmatized condition. We don't need to demonize people whose own demons are killing them. Jesus asks us to love, whether that's to hug your child or smile at a homeless person.

All three are now making good efforts at recovery. While there have been tough times, Jesus has shown me a more *just* way to love.

"Our greatest glory is not in never failing,
but in rising up every time we fail."
—Oliver Goldsmith

When You or Your Loved One Has Mental Illness

Turn, Lord, and deliver me; save me
because of your unfailing love.
—Psalm 6:4

My friend trembled, her tears spilling onto her lap. "It's no use," she confessed. "I just want to die." Her home had burned along with her beloved dogs and a cat. There wasn't much left, and she had no idea how to rebuild her life.

My heart broke for her, but I felt helpless. Years before, my own mother had tried to take her life and had called me first from another state to say goodbye. And now a dear friend was contemplating the same.

At both of those moments, panic rose in my throat. What could I say to convince a suicidal person that they were loved?

When a loved one suffers from mental health issues, large or small, panic explodes within us. We desperately want to help, yet if we're not trained professionals, we may feel awkward and clumsy. When a crisis arises, like the one with my friend, we feel urgency and responsibility.

In other people, mental or emotional problems only annoy or make it difficult to live with our loved ones. Again, we often feel helpless and don't know quite how to cope. Society's labels of crazy or nuts don't give us tools to soothe a situation or diffuse conflict. When someone we care about threatens to jump off a bridge, calling someone loony doesn't solve the problem.

Thankfully, God does know how we can deal with those with mental health challenges. In biblical times, deviant behavior was often attributed to the influence of demons. Nowadays, we know that our brains are complex organs that can go haywire. Psychologists know that more than anything, mental illness needs love and understanding.

When we feel helpless, prayer is our first defense. We ease anxiety by reassuring our loved ones of their safety in our presence and remaining close with them. When necessary, we also seek professional support. My mom survived after I prayed and listened to her. But I also called 911 and alerted her doctor.

Armed with knowledge and compassion, we can remain safe and still minister to someone who has lost hope. Much of mental illness is brought on by loss of hope. A soft and nonjudgmental voice communicates that they are valued. When we lend our loved one our listening ear, our hope and faith can help them get through their dark night.

I worried and prayed about my friend's dire situation. She was staying temporarily in a motel. I asked God what I might do to help. *Just be there for her,* the answer seemed to say. I sat with her, praying, listening to her fears, and loving her with my whole heart. That day, God carried us both.

"The strongest people are not those who show strength in front of the world but those who fight and win battles that others do not know anything about."

—Jonathan Harnisch

When Everything is Overwhelming

So do not fear, for I am with you; do not be dismayed,
for I am your God. I will strengthen you and help you;
I will uphold you with my righteous right hand.
—Isaiah 41:10

That autumn, our family was buried in grief. In the span of three months, several loved ones passed away. They included a favorite aunt, a treasured neighbor, a friend's tragic loss of a son, and my own mother. The day I had to choose Mom's funeral urn, my heart felt ripped in two.

I hadn't expected any of the losses. People said my loved ones had received their wings. But with my husband's ongoing kidney dialysis and heart problems, I wasn't just overwhelmed. I felt as if my own wings had been clipped.

Sorrow filled the air, but life does go on. And because my husband was ill, I was responsible for keeping things running. I didn't have time to grieve, with funerals to attend or plan, bills to pay. I was the main caregiver for my husband. I wanted to scream and run away.

In spite of modern conveniences, we can feel overwhelmed by our lives. Most households require two incomes to survive, so couples can feel like passing ships in the night. Parents feel more anxious and stressed about their children than ever before. Social media connects us but leads to loneliness. We often wish life would slow even as the rat race pushes us to run faster, do more, *be* more.

But God stands waiting for us to give up. Say what?

Yes, Jesus says to cast all our cares—that sinking feeling that we'll never get it all done—upon him. He doesn't promise that whatever overwhelms us will be easy or that we'll get a VIP pass to avoid all our obligations. As much as we wish to breeze through life without any pressure, God knows that our character develops (Romans 5:3) when we struggle to accomplish difficult things.

God promises us help and strength to do really hard stuff when we're ready to scream or throw in the towel. It's in that extra bit of energy when we're so tired. Determination and grit when juggling a million tasks. Comfort and the peace of God's love when coping with loss. When we're ready to fall down, maybe for the last time, the assurance that God will always prop us up. And remind us that God loves us with a furious passion.

That fall, I wasn't sure how I could possibly make it through such a terrible season. I was like a firefighter, running around extinguishing all the little blazes that cropped up. With each new spark, I thought my well had gone dry.

Yet Jesus carried me through every awful minute and even refilled me when I couldn't go on. I did some things very imperfectly, but with God's help, I did them. And whenever I feared I wasn't going to make it, I crawled beneath God's loving wings.

"Stop living in the land of why. There are no happy answers to 'why me?' 'why didn't I?' 'Why did I?' If you must ask any questions, ponder: 'How can I grow?' 'What's in my control to change?' 'What's a gain in my pain?'"

—Karen Salmansohn

When Fear is Winning

You came near when I called you, and you said, "Do not fear."
—Lamentations 3:57

Due to my chronic pain from the Late Effects of Polio (PPS), I've had to take strong medications for more than twenty-five years. The meds help me work as a writer and take care of my family. But when I received a new primary physician, I had to face facts: I'm not an addict, but I'm dependent on drugs that aren't beneficial as I age.

When the doctor suggested I wean myself off the pain meds, I felt skeptical. She referred me to a specialist who helps patients transition from opioids to a safer alternative. The specialist explained the process, and I froze. I'd need to be completely free of the meds for thirty-six hours before I could begin the buprenorphine replacement.

Terror ripped through me.

We set a date for the transition. The doctor assured me that she'd support me if I needed help during those opioid-free hours. I gulped but agreed.

Over the next few days, I tried to steel my resolve. In life, God had shown me that procrastination or delay only doubles my worry and anxiety. But every day I thought of reasons and excuses to back out. Change felt so scary.

Life often feels scary. We fear the unknown, whether it's an unknown land, an unknown person, a new job, school, or situation. Because we don't know what will happen, we often resort to *fight or flight* kind of fear. Sometimes, being afraid keeps us safe. We learn to have a deep respect for things that can hurt or destroy us. Most of the time, though, our fears are about what might or might not happen.

Our list of fears, rational and not so rational, might be one reason in the Bible God tells us not to fear more than one hundred times. In many different circumstances in both Old and New Testaments, God seems to be emphatic about not being afraid.

God must know that fear is a part of being human. And yet, when terror stalks, God asks us to stop and become aware of the divine presence. When we're scared out of our minds, Jesus comes alongside our quivering spirits and says, "Here, let me walk with you across this bed of burning coals."

Like a bestie who's with us through thick and thin, the Lord invites us to trade quaking-in-our-boots for stepping through the muck with the assurance that God isn't letting us go alone. When we're so frightened that we freeze, Jesus will carry us awhile by giving us the courage to face those fears. We'll be able to say, "Who can separate me from the love of God?" (Romans 8:39)

As the big day approached, I quit praying for a way out and began to pray for courage. I imagined the armor of God insulating me from the nasty withdrawal period. The new meds would be effective and safe, a gift from God. I arrived at the doctor's office, still apprehensive but with the sure knowledge that Jesus would carry me through.

"Courage is being scared to death but saddling up anyway."
—John Wayne

When You Suffer Alone

Also, if two lie down together, they will keep warm. But how can one keep warm alone?
—Ecclesiastes 4:11

When I was eight years old, I had a secret. My closest friends, Skeeter and Marcia, both attended the Catholic church. My family was staunchly Protestant. Skeet claimed she'd seen the Virgin Mary at the foot of her bed. In my house, icons and apparitions were forbidden. But I longed to have some sort of vision too.

We were on the swings at the school playground. Skeeter told us the story of her encounter with a translucent Mary, dressed in blue and hovering near the bed's footboard. We oohed and aahed, and then I blurted out, "My vision had Jesus all dressed in white. I thought I'd fall right out of bed!"

I'd made it all up and then lied to my friends.

I was terrified that my parents would find out about my hopes for a really cool apparition. And scared that these friends would discover my lie. For days, I suffered alone. I couldn't bring myself to confess to anyone, not even God.

Suffering isn't usually about hiding one's sins. We may have good reasons not to broadcast the reason we're hurting—some people are very private, and others keep their condition between them and God.

Misinformation or conflict can result in people we thought we knew abandoning us. Or if we've lived very different experiences than others in our relationships, that lack of connection separates us. If you aren't a parent, you might not understand a mom who's lost a child. And if you're blessed with children, you might question another person's decision to remain childless. Without walking a mile in someone else's moccasins, misunderstanding or stereotyping keeps us suffering alone.

God bakes into each of us the need for love, belonging, and acceptance. Along with urging us to stop being afraid, God says that we'll never be abandoned by our Lord. *I will never leave you or forsake you*, God says from Deuteronomy 31:6 and Hebrews 13:5. We may feel as if we're suffering alone, but God is *always* with us.

When utter loneliness overwhelms, we can look for God's presence wherever we are. Study verses about God being near or step outside and marvel at a butterfly's graceful flight. Pray and ask Jesus to show himself. Give someone a hug or a helping hand.

I never admitted my lie or told my folks that I wanted to see a vision. Instead, I embarked on a lifelong search for the Presence, the Comforter, the God who is love. The more I look, the more I feel God's sweet breath on my neck. I don't know if Jesus really dresses in white, but if he does, his robes must get dirty as he carries me through my dusty life.

"God has promised that whatever you face, you are not alone. He knows your pain. He loves you. And He will bring you through the fire."
—Sheila Walsh

When You're Disappointed

Awake, Lord! Why do you sleep? Rouse yourself!
Do not reject us forever. Why do you hide your
face and forget our misery and oppression?
—Psalm 44: 23-24

In my girlhood, I wanted to be a famous actress.

My adoptive father, apparently not wishing to see me hurt, always discouraged me from performing in plays. He knew not many roles call for a character with a polio-paralyzed arm.

Determined, I joined as many school or community plays as possible. I wrote plays, and one summer my bestie and I wrote and produced a melodrama. I played the heroine, Chastity, in *The Great Bottleneck Diamond*. The production at my high school was fun, and the performance was well-attended. The local paper did a write-up and featured my picture. I felt elated. Maybe I would be famous.

But the reviews left me devastated. Classmates who saw the performance asked why my arm didn't seem to move. One boy said he'd ask me out for a date if it wasn't for my disability. My father hugged me as I cried against his chest. But he reminded me that the world would be a cruel judge of anyone not considered normal.

Life can seem like one big disappointment after another. We dream of achieving a job or a life partner. We plan to travel abroad, buy a home, or accomplish a specific action. Our dream may be for a child or loved one, held with the hope of nurturing growth, confidence, or meaningful change. If our expectations don't materialize in the way or the time we've imagined, we feel let down. Hopes dashed, we ask ourselves what went wrong. We may stop trying altogether.

Yet while we're feeling disappointed, Paul tells us in Romans 6:5 that hope *doesn't* disappoint. How do we make sense of this?

Paul isn't telling us that disappointment is forbidden. But the hope that Paul describes doesn't come and go with our ups and downs. Paul's idea of hope means putting trust in a loving God through Jesus. Trust that holds up even when our worst fears happen. Trust that no circumstance can ever destroy.

Unfortunately, in life, we *will* have trouble. We can choose to be devastated and give up on life ever being good. Or we can trust that somehow, sometime in some way, God will work all things together for good.

Nobody likes to suffer. But suffering produces perseverance and perseverance character (Romans 5:3). If we're honest, we might see that our expectations are unreasonable, especially if those hopes are for someone *else* to change their ways. We may need to see that we can't change anyone except ourselves.

I felt disappointed after the melodrama when my acting aspirations deflated. My big dream to be famous popped like a cheap balloon. But God held me as closely as my dad did, soothing the sting of disappointment and nudging me to pour my creative energies into writing.

I'm still not famous, and it's no longer my dream. Instead, I write to proclaim my reliance on Jesus as he carries me to greater insights and helps me love God and others more and more.

**"We must accept finite disappointment,
but never lose infinite hope"**

—Martin Luther King Jr.

When Hope Feels Lost

Hope deferred makes the heart sick, but
a longing fulfilled is a tree of life.
—Proverbs 13:12

I've never met a little girl I'll call Belle. She's around nine or ten with owlish glasses and a stocking cap. And a terrible cancer. The poor kid has already suffered through more rounds of chemo and other treatments than most of us will in a lifetime. Her lips, cracked and riddled with sores, still break into an occasional smile.

I only know Belle through social media, but her mom reports on her daughter's condition. A few months ago, the prognosis was dire. Many prayers, including my own, shot to heaven for healing. Belle had battled back from the edge several times before. Yet now, Belle's mom sounded as if hope had gone missing altogether. Belle was sick. Her mom was sick with worry. Along with many others who prayed, I tried to lend a bit of hope.

Anyone who has been a caregiver likely understands how exhausted Belle's mom probably became after years of her daughter's cancer treatments. Tending to someone who can't manage is really hard. Whether it's a child, a spouse, or a relative, part of caring is helping the person keep hope alive.

Similarly, when faced with disaster in our own life, hope becomes much more important than simply keeping a positive outlook. Whether disease, divorce, or death is staring you down, hope—especially hope in a faithful, loving God—could be a matter of life and death.

Well-intentioned pray-ers sometimes equate hope with expectations for a certain answer to those prayers. If the outcome isn't what was prayed for, if healing doesn't come, or the miracle is late, we sometimes lose hope. Yet hope depends more on a deep knowing that God is love and that God is so *for* us.

Even those who face the most dangerous or cruel treatment can be sure that Jesus will carry them through the worst things—even those that result in disappointment or death. The hope that Christ's eternal love and his promise never to leave or forsake us allows us to believe that yes, weeping may last the terrible, awful, very long night, but that somehow, morning will come.

We don't have to like going through bad times. But Jesus invites us to come, cast every single care on him, and let his love carry us through.

I don't know if this last round of chemo will free Belle of cancer. Many people, including strangers like me, pray for healing. Belle stands upon the shoulders of those who pray, care, and love her. When she smiles, her whole face lights up as she says, "God is good."

"There is a light that shines in the darkness, which is only visible there."

—Barbara Brown Taylor

When It's Time to Let Go

And we know that in all things God works
for the good of those who love him, who have
been called according to his purpose.
—Romans 8:28

As a young woman, I thought my parents would last forever. After all, I'd known them all my life. But in my mid-twenties, my adoptive father developed a rare kidney disease. Years later, my husband had the same condition.

For more than a decade, hemodialysis kept my dad alive. Among the many crises along the way, in one near-death experience, Dad claimed he'd seen hell.

Dad recovered, and he changed. Never one to say much about faith, suddenly my father worried about heaven. He sat with me for hours, discussing life and death, salvation and grace. I didn't want to proselytize, but I told him about all the ways Jesus carried me. As a disabled woman, I needed courage and lots of it to compete in the workplace and in social life.

He nodded but politely said he was skeptical about Christianity in general. I smiled and said, "God loves you, Dad." He replied that our conversations gave him a lot to think about. But he knew he had little time left on earth.

When faced with impossible situations, it's human to want a positive outcome. The hope that we so carefully tend is too precious to toss away. Hope that the job will materialize, that somehow the rent money will appear, that our loved one will get well, and that someone out there will love us. Our deepest wants and needs grow roots, making it difficult to accept anything other than fulfillment.

Maybe that's why we say those who succumb to cancer fought hard or battled. Letting go of ideas, places, things, animals, or people is hard. Letting go can be so painful that we cling to our preferred story.

But God understands our pain. Jesus knows how tough it can be to walk this earth as a human. He suffers alongside us as we wrestle with letting go. He cares and comforts and strokes our hair, whispering, "Don't feel guilty. Let go."

More than merely commiserating, Jesus sympathizes as a person who endured great sorrow. Jesus can also help us get the timing right. Knowing when to let go of something or someone is more art than science. Our Lord will gently lead us to a place where we may still doubt ourselves, but we'll let go with more wisdom.

Only a few years later, my sister and I stood at my dad's hospital bedside, singing hymns and praying for him on his deathbed. As he breathed his last, he spoke. At first, I heard "water." Then I understood. My father prayed, "Our Father." Finally, I could let him go.

"To let go does not mean to get rid of. To let go means to let be. When we let be with compassion, things come and go on their own."

—Jack Kornfield

When You Experience Grace

For the law was given through Moses; grace
and truth came through Jesus Christ.
—John 1:17

When I was about fifteen, my dad grounded me for being late. This meant the school dance I'd anticipated, as well as the beautiful velveteen dress Mom sewed for me, was out. Dad thought he was teaching me a lesson. But I'd already learned to seek leniency from Mom.

I begged Mom to convince him to let me go to the dance.

Now, as a grandparent to three adorable kids, I see why Dad was so strict. My own four now-grown children do their best but still face the same balance between sternness and grace.

Parents, teachers, traffic cops, and judges, among others, struggle with this same problem—when to be consistent and when to be lenient. We don't want to be taken advantage of or allow others to get away with wrongdoing. Yet we recognize that we're human, that we make mistakes. It takes wisdom to figure out which is warranted, punishment or mercy.

Splitting the baby as King Solomon suggested often represents our indecisions over the law and grace. We make rules to help us live peaceably and efficiently. People break rules both large and small. Then we wrestle to find the next right thing to do.

Even God changes God's mind as He mercifully declared in Exodus 32:14. But in our society, clemency is often viewed as weak or unjust. We tend to think that those who show disregard for rules must be called out or punished in some way. We start to think of our loving God as a strict disciplinarian who doesn't accept excuses.

Often, we face natural consequences—touch a hot stove and burn our fingers. Consequences teach us if we're willing to learn. But God doesn't want us to avoid the divine the way we would a hot burner.

The truth is, God is love. When we suffer consequences, God only desires to heal, gain wisdom, and learn to love. When we experience the kind of grace where we are spared, like the baby King Solomon judged, we can't avoid receiving a healthy dose of fatherly love.

God's grace can be small or cosmic. The very air we breathe is grace, especially as we walk beside our Jesus. He reminds us that although we've screwed up, God's love is bigger than any mistake we can make. Grace exists to show God's love for all.

My dad thought he was being a good parent by forbidding me to attend that school dance. But after I went to him, apologized, and promised not to be late again, he softened. I could go after all, but he warned me not to be late. When I modeled my new dress for him, he smiled and said he loved me.

"God often takes a course for accomplishing His purposes directly contrary to what our narrow views would prescribe."

—John Newton

When You're Happy Anyway

Take delight in the Lord, and he will give
you the desires of your heart.
—Psalm 37:4

In my little life, I've faced disability from childhood polio, a failed first marriage, and many other disappointments. My three sons have battled substance use disorders, and my daughter has fragile health. I cared for my late husband in his kidney illness for more than ten years. Now I'm learning to be a widow.

But I consider myself happy. Sure, I have down times like everyone else. When people ask me why I'm a Christian, I don't answer that it's because of the promise of eternal life, although that's great. I'm a Christian because Jesus makes my life better.

When I watched my husband pass away from a massive stroke, Jesus sat beside me, sharing his bottomless love. When I get impatient in traffic, Jesus is there to calm me down and remind me that the cars hold people that God loves as much as he loves me. When I'm shaking with fear as they're wheeling me to the operating room, Jesus won't leave me alone. If I had to bear these burdens by myself, I would definitely be unhappy.

Rarely do any of us get through this life without some calamity. Dreams fail to materialize. Friends betray us. Our loved ones get sick and die. Even our culture preaches that without more stuff, status, or security, we can't really be happy. God has to remind us often to stop fearing, stop lashing out, stop our tendencies toward greed and malice, sloth and avarice. We want what we don't have or think that the same kind of grass is better just because it's in our neighbor's lawn.

Maybe that's why Jesus says that in this life we will have trouble (John 16:33). But the other piece of that Scripture is harder to remember, *but take heart, for I have overcome the world.*

For me, overcoming the world means that Jesus rides shotgun wherever I go. Sometimes that means God is comforting me, holding my hand, or carrying me across a raging river. Other times, Jesus gently reminds me that love takes action and encourages me to live out my love.

When I reach for Jesus' hand or meditate on his words, I can say I'm happy. I'm very grateful that my troubles pale in comparison to the giants of the faith. Most of all, I'm thankful for a God who loves me completely and helps me love others as myself.

Counting our blessings isn't a bad idea when we're down and depressed and don't see a way out. Feasting on nature or appreciating a stranger's smile can lift a bad mood. Choosing happiness helps us remember that Jesus is always carrying us through whatever we face.

"There is only one happiness in this life, to love and be loved."

—George Sand

When God Carries You, Let Him!

But the fruit of the Spirit is love, joy, peace, forbearance, kindness, goodness, faithfulness, gentleness and self-control. Against such things there is no law.
—Galatians 5:22-23

One of my darkest times was in the summer of 1977, when my little sister got married.

She came home from a Christian college with a few of her friends. At that time, I was a lonely divorcee, teaching public school art. I felt miserable and to provoke these Christians, I said I was interested in tarot cards. For the cool illustrations, mind you. But they recoiled as if I'd bitten the head off a snake. I laughed at them.

It was the height of the Jesus Movement. What patsies they were, talking about Jesus and studying The Word. I dared not tell anyone that I hated my life and only wanted someone to love.

Fast forward to today in the twenty-first century. Some have hidden their anguish, certain that God isn't interested in them. Some deconstruct or leave the church due to trauma. Others decide God doesn't exist.

Does that God-shaped hole keep you awake at night? Or whisper in the back of your mind? Maybe your prayers haven't been answered—Uncle Bob got away with molesting children, Aunt

Peggy died from cancer, your urgent prayer request didn't produce the hoped-for miracle.

Perhaps you think church members are hypocritical, so you avoid every church. If all you hear is other "believers" pointing out your mistakes, you might wonder why you don't experience God in your life. You know you're supposed to love God, but in your day-to-day it feels hollow like an unreachable gift.

Yeah, me too.

I was saved long before I grew to really love the Lord. Those who urged me to believe and accept salvation meant well. I wanted to love Jesus and be a good Christian. But I sure didn't experience that love in my ordinary life.

It took a lot of prayer and God-with-skin-on encounters, but gradually God became real to me. I began to see Jesus in every person I knew. I looked for and saw God's love everywhere. I've stumbled many times along the way, but the more I love others, the more God's love opens my heart, filling that empty place.

Many times, my prayers aren't answered in the way I wish—the rent gets raised anyway, my husband died from his stroke. Even my prayers for physical healing of my paralysis from polio haven't delivered a jaw-dropping miracle, although I still pray for one.

These days, unlike the seventies, I don't scoff at Christianity, and tarot cards aren't allowed in my life. If I've learned anything, it's that Jesus' love really does bring peace that passes all understanding. And when God offers to carry me through the rough patches, I let him. I hope you'll let God carry you, too.

"God loves each one of us as if there were only one of us to love."
—Augustine

Made in the USA
Columbia, SC
09 April 2026

81546669R00116